BRAIN GAMES®

CROSSWORD
Challenge

Publications International, Ltd.

Let's get social!

 @Publications_International

@PublicationsInternational

@BrainGames.TM

www.pilbooks.com

Challenge Ready?

Grab a pencil (or pen) and get ready! The following crossword puzzles touch on a variety of subjects, including sports, movies, music, places, and more. Don't worry if you get stuck. Answers are conveniently located at the back of the book for when you need a hint or have strained your brain enough.

The puzzles may be difficult, but there are many ways you can solve these challenges. First of all, always work in pencil, because you never know when an answer you're "pretty" sure about ends up not fitting into the greater scheme of the puzzle. Also, always try to solve the fill-in- the-blank clues first; they are generally an easy access point. You can try solving two- and three-letter, plural, and abbreviated clues first, too. These will hint at some of the longer, more difficult clues.

AMERICAN FOLK TALES

ACROSS

1. Balkan native
5. A helping hand
8. Any of the Galapagos
12. Base of Hawaiian poi
13. Card game based on crazy eights
14. "Mister Roberts" setting
15. "Amo, amas, ___"
16. Shudder-inducing
18. Paul Bunyan's awesome bovine companion
20. "Fiddlesticks!"
21. "Do the Right Thing" director Spike
22. Ham's device
25. Bk. before Numbers
26. Badly lit
29. Niagara Falls legend about a young Indian woman
32. "Sister Act" sister
33. Gave dinner to
34. Big name in cameras
35. "One Day ___ Time"
36. Not hers or his
37. Legendary logger and Forest Service warden
44. As a lark
45. Any NATO member to another

46. Belfry sound
47. Athlete's outfit
48. Buck or ram
49. Girl in a Salinger story
50. Actress Thompson in "Back to the Future"
51. Coup d'___ (uprising)

DOWN

1. Blind guess
2. The genus that contains alpacas
3. Baghdad native
4. Poll worker's request
5. Anything whatever
6. About, in legal memos
7. There's one in "fishhook"
8. Debatable topic
9. Brake pad
10. Prom ride, for short
11. Climber's goal
17. Near-final hour
19. More frequently than is good
22. Watergate monogram
23. Nonprofessional sports org.
24. Annoying racket
25. Inc., in England
26. Hagar's creator Browne
27. Equal: Prefix
28. Peak, for short
30. Scared

4

31. Title incorrectly
35. Deft and active
36. Old Greek region
37. Mock
38. French islands
39. Bowie's rock genre

40. Bride's month
41. Bedframe part
42. Ceramic jug
43. Bolshevik's denial

ANSWERS ON PAGE 228.

WHAT'S COOKING

ACROSS

1. "Geek Squad" worker
5. "Indent" key
8. Airport boarding place
12. Salvation ___ (where many NFL players volunteer)
13. DVD predecessor
14. "Green" emotion
15. Disquiet
17. Alaskan Gold Rush town
18. "My Big Fat Greek Wedding" star Vardalos
19. ___ populi (popular opinion)
21. Breakfast order
28. It comes before "di-dah"
29. "Do Ya" rock band
30. Actor Flynn with a sword
31. Eye part with color
33. Catch-all term
35. "Buona ___" (Italian "Good evening")
36. Bedtime for many
38. Bath fixture
40. Chi. Clock setting
41. Musical toys
44. First lady
45. "Madama Butterfly" sash

46. Empty expanse
49. Pupil's writing need
54. Bali or Capri
55. Equals, in math
56. About in legalspeak
57. Blacken lightly
58. Denial from de Gaulle
59. Not at port

DOWN

1. Ancient cross
2. Coastal eagle
3. Meas. on IKEA boxes
4. "Laughing" critter
5. Stand for an idiot box
6. Athletes often tear it
7. Alla ___ (music notation)
8. Boomers' kids
9. "Feliz ___ Nuevo!" ("Happy New Year!")
10. "I really appreciate that," while texting
11. One of two that view
16. "Newsweek" rival
20. Poem that honors
21. Capri pants features
22. 1970's batting champ Rod
23. "Watch on the ___," 1941 Lillian Hellman play
24. Big-win, high-odds game

25. El ___ (Spanish artist)
26. Growth on English moors
27. Bed frame strips
32. Driver doing 90, say
34. Use a scalpel on
37. Network that aired "Jersey Shore"
39. Crib occupant
42. Georgia pie nut
43. Bone below the knee

46. "___ for Vengeance" (Grafton novel)
47. Ending for "verb" or "malt"
48. Dock workers' union
50. "___ y Plata" (Montana motto)
51. Appliance buttons
52. Portland's st.
53. Hawaii's Mauna ___

ANSWERS ON PAGE 228.

SIDE DISHES

ACROSS

1. Church robes
5. Ghostly pale
8. A millipede has many
12. "Your majesty"
13. "Boola Boola" collegian
14. A hodgepodge
15. Anti-workplace discrimination org.
16. Automated Web browser
17. Apple-picking season
18. Veggie side dish
21. Big name in early supercomputers
22. "The Good Wife" fig.
23. Like a hot fudge sundae
25. "The dog ___ my homework"
26. Be human, according to saying
29. Hooters at night
30. "Game of Thrones" beverage
31. Cutesy letter closer
32. "A Farewell to Arms" conflict, briefly
33. "___ Wiedersehen!"
34. Burger side order
35. "Special" military missions
36. Filmed, as a movie

37. Side dish of spuds from the oven
43. Not a fan of
44. ___ League college
45. "Golden Rule" word
46. Dust ___: tiny house critter
47. "Fantasia" frame, e.g.
48. Govt. labor board
49. Sun, for one
50. Hitherto
51. Adds highlights at the salon

DOWN

1. "Hold on ___!"
2. Place, in legalese
3. Side dish of healthy spears
4. Makes safe
5. Like doorways of haunted houses
6. Botanical balm
7. Garden fertilizer
8. Diet, informally
9. Airline from Israel
10. ___ monster (large lizard)
11. "Gone!" at auctions
19. Graduation time, often
20. Abbr. in some Quebec addresses
23. Pai ___ (Chinese gambling game)

8

24. Cry of pain in the comics
25. '80s prime-time alien
26. Highway warning sign
27. Fish eggs, or a kind of deer
28. Prescriptions, for short
30. Favorable sign
31. Rich, as a voice
33. Especially relevant

34. Fed. mortgage insurer
35. Basket twig
36. Fashion plate's forte
37. Aries animals
38. "Consider it done"
39. "___ girl!" ("Nice job!")
40. "I'm ___ it"
41. Ah, "to be" in Paris!
42. Cries out loud

ANSWERS ON PAGE 228.

ONE OF THE STAR WARS

ACROSS

1. Apprentice of Qui-Gon Jinn in 13-Across
9. Doc's org.
10. Well-run operation, metaphorically
11. Gunslinger's mark
12. Urban play area
13. Episode I of the "Star Wars" franchise, with "The"
17. Case for a lawyer
19. Messing of "Will and Grace"
21. West Florida port
23. Public notices
24. Actor who played 1-Across

DOWN

2. Use dynamite
3. "Be careful!"
4. Annoy persistently
5. Vocalist John
6. Laertes's sister, in "Hamlet"
7. Feedback
8. Short sleep
12. River known for a WWI battle
14. One of a bug's pair
15. Final stage
16. Go by
17. Computer logo
18. Gaping fissure
20. "Nice job!"
22. Ending of many Web site names

ANSWERS ON PAGE 228.

IT'S ALL IN HOW YOU READ IT

ACROSS

1. "The King of Queens" actress Remini

5. "___ good turn daily" (Boy Scouts slogan)

8. Lots

12. "Alice's Restaurant" singer Guthrie

13. Caterer's coffee server

14. David and Goliath's battlefield

15. Former SNL star Kristen

16. "Give ___ break!"

17. Aloha State bird

18. Where you live—or bully next door?

21. Author Chinua Achebe, by birth

22. "Homeland" agcy.

23. Bit of statuary

26. DVD forerunner

27. Bacon feature

30. "Could be trouble!"

31. How-to letters

32. "Fiddlesticks!"

33. "Didn't need to hear that!"

34. Sugar snap

35. Came up

36. Archer's asset

37. The Gay Nineties, e.g.

38. Below the level of awareness—or thinking about a long sandwich?

44. Burkina ___ (African nation)

45. "Teletubbies" fan

46. Prefix meaning "skin"

47. Allowed to mellow

48. Burgundy summer

49. Ecto's opposite

50. Air Force outpost

51. "Gidget" star Sandra

52. Ex-QB Flutie

DOWN

1. Croquet play area

2. Huron neighbor

3. Et ___ ("and others")

4. Greedy—or keep actress Lillian all to yourself?

5. Beloved Disney elephant

6. "Got Milk?" ad partner

7. Complete lawlessness

8. Birthplace of Columbus

9. Alternative spread

10. Merry Men unit

11. Junk, to a sailor

19. "Game of Thrones" cable channel

20. Grafton's "___ for Homicide"

23. "Boy king" of Egypt

24. Bit of resistance
25. Bourbon ruler
26. By way of
27. Egg ___ Yung
28. "A Midsummer Night's Dream" disguise
29. "That'll be ___ day!"
31. Kicked downstairs
32. Like pigtails—or recognized bikini top?
34. Apt rhyme for "flick"
35. Boomerang's path

36. "Humble" dwelling
37. Beauty expert Lauder
38. "Beowulf," for one
39. Doesn't allow to gather dust
40. Brief reminder
41. Prefix meaning "wine"
42. Hindu language
43. Air pollutant
44. "The ___ Four" (The Beatles)

1	2	3	4		5	6	7		8	9	10	11
12					13				14			
15					16				17			
18				19				20				
			21				22					
23	24	25				26				27	28	29
30					31				32			
33				34				35				
		36				37						
	38	39			40				41	42	43	
44				45				46				
47				48				49				
50				51				52				

13

ANSWERS ON PAGE 229.

MERYL STREEP MOVIES

ACROSS

1. Comfy footwear, for short
5. "What, me worry?" magazine
8. Film-rating grp.
12. Brief brouhaha
13. Bar brew, briefly
14. "A Farewell to ___" (Hemingway)
15. One's 'hood, for short
16. "That's life!"
18. Tommy Lee Jones and Steve Carell co-starred with Streep in this 2012 romantic comedy-drama
20. "Animal Farm" setting
21. Belgian 1914 battle river
22. "Thriller" follow-up
25. Playwright Stoppard
27. Bite-size appetizer
30. Streep plays vacationing housewife Ellen Martin in this 2019 biographical comedy-drama with Gary Oldman and Antonio Banderas
34. "The Kitchen God's ___"
35. Comstock find

36. "Jeanne d'Arc," for one: abbr.
37. Extremely narrow shoe marking
40. "Goody Two Shoes" singer Adam
42. Streep is British activist Emmeline Pankhurst in this 2015 historical drama
46. Comfortably off
47. Burden
49. "Aphrodite" sculptor
50. "___ Wiedersehen" (goodbye)
51. 100 percent, as gold
52. It's right on a map?
53. Basketball official
54. Do a stevedore's job

DOWN

1. Bill Gates's ISP
2. Aquarium beauty
3. Baja resort area, familiarly
4. "The 39 ___" (Hitchcock movie)
5. Love-letter signoff
6. Each, informally
7. Cheese farm
8. Small electric generator
9. Theatrical handouts
10. "My Cup Runneth Over" singer

11. Donkey or burro relative
17. "Whether ___ nobler in the mind to suffer...": Hamlet
19. "At Last" singer James
22. "Incidentally" in a chat room
23. Fish on a sushi menu
24. Fails to pay back, as a loan
26. 6 on a phone pad
28. "Heartbreaker" singer Benatar
29. Grabbed a bite
31. Candidate's handout

32. Carry away
33. "The Pilgrim" painter Magritte
38. At the back of the boat
39. Bustling with noise or excitement
41. Alternatives to moonroofs
42. "Buona ___" (Italian "Good evening")
43. In unison, musically
44. Carpenter's fastener
45. 100 cents, in Europe
46. Easy to miss
48. Attach a patch, say

ANSWERS ON PAGE 229.

SEE CRUISE

ACROSS

1. Tom Cruise title role of 1996

9. 31-day mo.

10. On edge

11. Toss of the dice

12. Mother lode

13. 1983 Tom Cruise where he danced in his skivvies

17. Get all decked out

19. Bran benefit

21. Starting today

23. Terrier's bark

24. 1999 Tom Cruise film with Nicole Kidman

DOWN

2. All fired up

3. Scenic transport

4. "Braveheart" star Gibson

5. Barely make it

6. "Just think!"

7. What's going on

8. Sunday speaker

12. Like cooked hot dogs

14. Initial phase

15. Little ones

16. Actor's reading material

17. "Platoon" Oscar nominee Willem

18. Bone connector

20. Linda Ronstadt's "Blue ___"

22. Become a better half

ANSWERS ON PAGE 229.

COMFY AT HOME

ACROSS

1. Child in the care of a guardian
5. Bad sound for a balloonist
8. Axe handle
12. Antioxidant berry
13. Light brew, for short
14. "Bearded" flower
15. $20 bill dispensers
16. Disco-era kid
17. Dennis the Menace's friend
18. Relaxing wooden seat
21. Don Ho's instrument, informally
22. Fond du ___ (Wisconsin city)
23. A journalistic "W"
26. "___ Miserables" (Broadway musical)
27. Contents of jewel cases
30. Down-home wood burner
33. Emcee's aid
34. Cap, as on spending
35. Ancient Aegean land
36. Boxer's poke
37. "Dune" co-composer Brian
38. It makes for a cozy night's sleep

45. Get a new mortgage, informally
46. ___ room (place for air hockey)
47. Big party
48. It serves Jerusalem
49. Picasso's year
50. French river or department
51. Charlotte Bronte's "Jane ___"
52. Auctioneer's batch
53. Dental image

DOWN

1. WWII woman
2. Deeds, in Latin
3. Freeway entrance or exit
4. "Do not" follower, on a closed-door sign
5. Impish dust sprinkler
6. Be the first act
7. Dinner-plate garnish
8. Soprano's top note
9. "Carmen" song
10. Concluded, in Cannes
11. Old emperor of Russia
19. "___ and the Bee," 2006 film
20. Oleg of fashion
23. Keystrokes meas.
24. ___ polloi
25. "And so on" letters

18

26. Atty.'s degree
27. "Vaya ___ Dios"
28. 506, in old Rome
29. Sailor's realm
31. Politically left-leaning
32. Handyman's tote
36. 8-pointer in Scrabble
37. Disney World's ___ Center
38. At no cost to you

39. Difficult to grasp, as an elongated fish
40. A long way off
41. Mini-Vegas
42. Lion's den
43. Bones, anatomically
44. Curds and ___ (Muffet's meal)

ARTHURIAN LEGEND

ACROSS

1. Cavern comeback
5. Round Table king
11. Bird on Canadian dollars
12. Cherry red
13. Peevish temper
14. Made like a mob
15. A few or a lot
16. Like a needle's eye
17. Rock containing crystals
19. Chunk of history
22. Theatrical backdrop
24. Mason partner
26. Put on, as a uniform
27. South American tubers
28. Astrological Ram
30. Turbaned sage
31. Good bud
32. Demolish, as a car
34. Pickle or jam
35. Of that ___ (of the same sort)
38. Desirable things
41. But, in Bonn
42. Lake Itasca, for the Mississippi
43. Dervish, for one
44. Lancelot or Galahad
45. Crafts cohort

DOWN

1. 1814 exile isle
2. Fountain throwaway
3. Object of the medieval quest
4. It comes after twelve
5. Bitter tasting
6. Controlled, as a horse
7. Greece's foe in "The Iliad"
8. Broadway smash
9. Get value from
10. "Curse you, ___ Baron!"
16. Clancy or Cruise
18. Ireland alias
19. The sword in the stone
20. Give in to wanderlust
21. Standards org.
22. Do some bartering
23. Actor Michael of "Juno"
25. "The Music Man" state
29. Bit of embroidery
30. Gold is one: Abbr.
33. First stage
34. Arctic hazard, for short
36. Southpaw's pitching arm
37. "Me and Bobby McGee" writer Kristofferson
38. Beg a favor

39. Heir, but not an heiress   **41.** Hungry-bear link
40. Fashion's Anna

FIND THE CITY

ACROSS

1. Environmental condition in a Peruvian city?
8. Hose in a shell, once
13. Footsteps sound
14. Under-the-sink pipe
15. 1991 Steve Martin film set in Calif.
16. In need of an update
17. ICU part
18. Subject to change
20. To put something somewhere
22. "I get it now" sounds
23. Agent of Uncle Sam
24. Big name in health plans
26. Hugs, in a letter
27. Amuse greatly
30. Driving reversals
33. "Fifth Beatle" Yoko
34. Diplomatic negotiations
36. Mo. for an apple festival
37. Cookie holder
38. "I wish I were an ___ Mayer wiener"
42. Swinging around
44. Alley Oop's abode
45. "The Language of Clothes" author Alison
46. Classic mouthwash

49. Taking too much, for short
50. Fence in
51. Dandelions, e.g.
52. Lack the courage to include a Nevada city?

DOWN

1. A little better than average
2. "Weekend Edition Sunday" host ___ Hansen
3. "Let ___ where it is"
4. Tool similar to a pickax
5. GI address letters
6. Black sticky stuff
7. Original form of a word
8. Strong cravings
9. "Call My Name" jazz singer James
10. Try to seize, as the gold ring
11. Mexican city found in an old warship?
12. Racer's swimwear
19. Big name in rental trucks
21. Zero, in soccer scores
25. "Hop on!"
27. Norwegian city seen not keeping up?
28. Count in

29. Pennsylvania city found in a circle of friends?
31. Bout ender, for short
32. Destroyer attacked in Aden in Oct., 2000
35. Fished with a hook
37. 1970s supermodel Cheryl

39. "Gigi" star Leslie
40. French message-carrying boat
41. Adjust one's watch
43. Air force?
47. Actress and comic Gasteyer
48. '70s tape player

 ANSWERS ON PAGE 230.

DIRECTED BY CLINT EASTWOOD

ACROSS

1. Eastwood directed and stars as Preacher in 1985's "__ Rider," the highest-grossing Western of the decade

5. About-to-be-grads or AARP members, briefly

8. Bickering bout

12. Classic '80s sports car

13. "I'm amazed!"

14. 175-year-old canal

15. It goes up in a downpour

17. "A __ formality!"

18. This 1992 Eastwood-directed Western won wide acclaim and four Academy Awards, including Best Picture

20. 1938 Sartre novel

23. Big __ (David Ortiz nickname)

24. 911 respondent, briefly

25. Get the wrong signals from

28. Eastwood produced, directed, and acted (as a master jewel thief) in this 1997 political action thriller

32. Pastry chef's forms

33. Pitching number with a decimal

34. Alternative to "ja"

35. Having no pattern

38. Though named after a muscle car, this 2008 Clint Eastwood drama is not a racing movie

41. A great many

42. Dish-drying cloth

46. Melancholy woodwind

47. "The Lord of the Rings" tree being

48. This 1988 Eastwood-directed movie is a fond tribute to jazz saxophonist Charlie Parker

49. 'Sesame Street' regular

50. Agcy. for narcs

51. British men of title

DOWN

1. More, in music scores

2. A slot machine has one

3. Arced, soft throw

4. Beige shades

5. Scale syllables

6. Candy in a tube

7. Permanent marker brand

8. Minor-league, maybe

9. Watched ahead of time

10. "Billion" suffix
11. "Happy Days" extra
16. Chicago-to-Toronto dir.
19. ("I'm shocked!")
20. A type of tide
21. Both (prefix)
22. Warren or Romney, e.g.
25. Geog. high points
26. "Flying" start
27. $\frac{1}{8}$ fluid ounce
29. Mathematical collection that isn't closed
30. Au __ (with milk)

31. Not seen
35. Calf roper's rope
36. Kitchen intruder
37. Neophytes, in slang
38. Amount of goop
39. After-bath garment
40. Thinker Descartes
43. Big name in video games
44. Exhibit one's humanity
45. Church of the Mormons: abbr.

ANSWERS ON PAGE 230.

GOING TOW TO TOE

ACROSS

1. The act of putting fruit in gin?
8. Like many a wrestler
9. Clean plate comment
10. Homes on wheels, for short
11. Not in the least difficult
13. Ride an iceberg?
16. Please the palate
19. Fanatic
21. In the zone
23. Repeated word in "The Trolley Song"
24. Hunger pang due to a piece of froot cereal?

DOWN

1. Fencing sword
2. Tended
3. "We'll see"
4. Earl Grey, e.g.
5. Taking time off
6. Daytime TV drama
7. All night flight
12. Brief disagreement
13. "Hit the road!"
14. 1979 Bette Midler film
15. Way back
17. One in a set of steps
18. Russian country house
20. Get dressed
22. London lavatory

ANSWERS ON PAGE 230.

ROCKET MAN

ACROSS

1. Author of the book that 14-Across is based on
5. The best pair in poker
8. Campers, for short
9. Per item cost
11. Vote for one not on the ballot
13. Florida metropolis
14. John Glenn was a character in this 1983 film
17. Awaiting a pitch
19. Laundry room vat
22. Election decider, perhaps
24. ATM access code
25. "Happy Days" extra
26. He played John Glenn in 14-Across

DOWN

1. Lose on purpose
2. It may be guided or heat-seeking
3. Good for something
4. G-man employer
6. Fine tableware
7. Old West lawman
10. Gasoline dispensers
12. Not at all
14. "All done!"
15. "Hello! I'm ..." badge
16. In good condition
18. "I do" sayer
20. "Bye for now!"
21. Additional remuneration
23. Off the wall

ANSWERS ON PAGE 231.

MOVIE REMAKES

ACROSS

1. "A fickle food," per Emily Dickinson
5. "Sesame Street" network
8. PC scrolling key
12. Ancient Egyptians held it sacred
13. Christmas tree sales site
14. 100 cents, in Europe
15. It offers goods under a canvas shelter
17. Apply paint crudely
18. Beyoncé is Nala in this 2019 remake of the first Disney animated film with an original story
20. Barrett of the original Pink Floyd
21. "Cola" lead-in
22. A long way off
25. It means "fire bowl" in Japanese
28. Bill Murray is the voice of Baloo, a good-natured bear, in this 2016 remake of the Kipling tales
32. Repudiate
33. "Amazing Grace" verse ender
34. Chatted with online, briefly
35. "I pity the fool!" speaker

38. Bradley Cooper and Lady Gaga star in this third remake of the 1937 film about an aspiring actress and the actor who helps her (2018)
42. Edmonton's province, briefly
43. Building wing
45. It can get you in on the ground floor
46. Milking parlor sound
47. Body chill
48. Breath mint in a roll, informally
49. "Happy Days" setting
50. Crow's-nest sighting

DOWN

1. Appropriate
2. Act as a getaway driver, say
3. Ho Chi ___ Trail
4. "Blue Bloods" actor Will
5. Bagpiper's pattern
6. Arizona necktie
7. Crate marking, maybe
8. Human-powered taxi
9. Llamas' cousins
10. Controlled substance
11. San Francisco's ___ Hill
16. Admirably crafty
19. Expensive cut of beef
22. Big initials in bouquets

23. Fish wrapped in nori
24. Electric-current blocker
25. "The Time Machine" author's monogram
26. Do groundbreaking work
27. "I Like ___" ('50s campaign slogan)
29. Fruit-filled pastry
30. Eye part that holds the iris
31. Rhyming nickname for Obama
35. Old PC standard

36. A homer provides at least one
37. Add up
38. Succulent with many uses
39. Show that launched Kelly Clarkson's career, familiarly
40. Capital of Latvia
41. "Common" or "proper" word
42. General's assistant: abbr.
44. "Game of Thrones" patriarch

ANSWERS ON PAGE 231.

FOWL LANGUAGE

ACROSS

1. Doubletalk
8. Response to "You won't believe this!"
9. Seafood cookout
10. Intercom speaker
12. "Born In the ___"
13. Stand-up comedian Jeff
17. Hesitation sounds
18. Blockhead
20. Backyard basking spot
22. Footwear pair
23. Sheepless shepherdess

DOWN

2. "The joke's ___!"
3. Business, facetiously
4. Helper for Santa
5. Elizabeth I's favorite
6. Not clocked in
7. ATM feature
8. What to do
11. Halloween prop
13. Stocking style or angling device
14. Puts on the board
15. Evade, with "out of"
16. Dashes through the snow
18. Reside
19. "I give up!"
21. CIA counterpart

ANSWERS ON PAGE 231.

CHARACTERS WE LOVE

ACROSS

1. On ___ (as a gamble)
5. Hogwarts mail carriers
9. Blocked from view
12. Cantina munchie
13. "Here comes trouble"
14. Academic URL ender
15. "Once ___ a time..."
16. Modern recording option
17. Abbr. after many a general's name
18. Teen sleuth of books, movies, TV
20. "Merry" month
21. A place to go in London?
22. "Sorry Not Sorry" singer Lovato
24. Bayou cuisine
27. Exhaust
30. Short nail
31. Take a load off
32. Aardvark's dinner
33. Africa's westernmost nation
35. Behave furtively
36. Ball-shaped cheese
37. Big name in averages
38. Award bestowed by the queen, for short

40. Legendary archer-bandit of English folklore
45. Fork out
46. State decisively
47. "Python" Eric
48. Make a mistake
49. Bloods or Crips
50. Cut of pork
51. Born as, for women
52. Art Deco artist
53. A.k.a. Cupid

DOWN

1. Astonish
2. Bear in the big chair
3. "The dismal science," briefly
4. Decided by reasoning
5. Perform better than
6. Electric-fan sound
7. Brief rave review
8. "Psycho" scene setting
9. Friend of Harry and Ron
10. Brainstormer's spark
11. Customs fee
19. "Round ___ virgin..."
23. "___, back on the farm..."
24. "60 Minutes" network
25. Is plural?
26. Bronte heroine
27. "Shop ___ you drop"

28. Acting guru Hagen
29. Cluck of disapproval
31. Russian tea urn
34. Grease monkey's workplace
35. Junior, to Senior
37. Funeral music
38. Transparent

39. Like Mother Hubbard's cupboard
41. Like a proposer's knee
42. Annoying smell
43. A little of this and a little of that
44. Bear lairs

THE HALF-MARATHON

ACROSS

1. Start of a quip about running a half-marathon
8. "Puh-lease!"
9. Painter Picasso
10. More of the quip
12. Hot spot
14. Win big, with "up"
16. More of the quip
18. One way to buy an item
21. "Good job!"
22. Cheat on
23. End of the quip

DOWN

1. ___ many words
2. The Gold Coast, today
3. Where drinks are on the host
4. Tall president, for short
5. Perform like Gregory Hines
6. It goes out on the beach
7. Carol, for example
11. "Madam Secretary" star Téa
12. Drink a bit
13. Wealthy contributor
15. IRA, e.g.
17. Slo-mo mammal
19. "Star Trek" genre
20. Bride's attire
22. Prefix with heel

ANSWERS ON PAGE 232.

HELLO, AUSSIES

ACROSS

1. Casino receipts
5. Wide gap in type
12. "Survivor" immunity token
13. Egg-laying mammal
14. Blue, in Berlin
15. Christmas tree decoration
16. Indigenous word for a creek that runs during the rainy season only
18. "La ___" (Debussy piece)
19. Agcy. that aids start-ups
20. "Beg pardon!"
21. It might give you a jump-start
22. Freezing prefix
23. Cranky
25. "Golden Boy" dramatist Clifford
27. Clasp hands
28. ___ Lumpur, Malaysian capital
29. Electric fan sound
30. Dune buggy, e.g.
31. Pate de ___ gras
32. 911 call responder
35. A grand slam home run gets four

36. Where "G'day!" is heard
38. Satchel for guys
40. Abbr. on egg cartons
41. Stressed
42. Be alive with
43. "The Simpsons" principal
44. ___ on the wrist

DOWN

1. "They Call Me MISTER ___!" (1970 film)
2. "Whose Line Is It Anyway?" feature
3. Adorable Australian
4. Month preceding Rosh Hashanah
5. Cheap cigar, slangily
6. Grauman's Chinese Theatre, formerly ___
7. All-male bash
8. Poe's "The Narrative of Arthur Gordon ___"
9. Part of a gorilla costume
10. Wedge-shaped
11. Lost sheep, to a lawyer
13. Mardi Gras sandwiches, informally
17. Artery from the heart
22. "Simpsons" frame
23. President who resigned during the fall of Saigon

24. A missing pencil may be behind one
25. Australian wilderness
26. Dan Brown's "The ___ Code"
27. Polished, as shoes
28. Destinies, to some
29. Humdinger

31. Strong suit
32. '50s four-wheeled flop
33. Euripides play
34. "Little" Chaplin role
36. Nora of "SNL"
37. Cashews or filberts
39. Autograph-seeker's need

WILD ANIMALS

ACROSS

1. Soothing, like ointment?
8. Unexpected defeat
9. Was taken down a peg
10. Way back when
11. Steakhouse selection
12. Prepare to dress for the forum?
16. Bochco legal drama
18. Not in custody
20. Press release
21. Awaiting a pitch
22. May registration?

DOWN

1. Semisoft cheese
2. "Don't worry about it"
3. Numerous, slangily
4. Completely confused
5. Highly skilled
6. Ship sunk at Pearl Harbor
7. Kind of crew
12. Deep ravines
13. Babe in a maternity ward
14. Off with permission
15. Crossed the threshold
17. About the moon
18. Ancient Mexican
19. Puzzle cube inventor

ANSWERS ON PAGE 232.

IN THE LONG RUN

ACROSS

1. Alphabet firsts
5. Very long race
9. Of a child
10. Inuit knife
11. Green hopper
12. Category of physique: 2 wds.
17. Type widths
19. Harmless skin defect
20. ___ Fleming, 007 creator
21. Newspaper employee
24. No longer in the workforce: abbr.
25. Covered in
26. Sun: prefix
27. Celtics' hometown
30. City with the Big Ben
31. Machu Picchu citizen
32. City founded by Pizarro
33. Ancient France
34. Useless gesture
38. Chart-topping song
39. Cereal container
40. Shelter org.
41. Shrimp catcher: 2 wds.
44. Exploded
45. IRS agent: abbr.
46. Capital of Zimbabwe
47. 5k track event
48. Thunderstruck

DOWN

1. Subsequently
2. Ecological community
3. Fastener
4. "I ___ not!"
5. Big leagues: abbr.
6. Less polite
7. First film Superman
8. Disapproving sound
13. Overdue
14. Produce
15. Barbecue area
16. Conclude with: 2 wds.
18. Sweater fabric
22. Of base 8
23. Summer shade
24. Of the kidneys
26. Good friend
27. Wide bay
28. Radio studio sign: 2 wds.
29. Old Roman shields
30. Ignited
32. Opulence
34. Jane ___, actress
35. Spouse's parent
36. "___ you are!"
37. Swerved off course momentarily
39. Image quality issue
42. Angkor ___, temple in Cambodia
43. Not just any
44. Victoria's Secret product

ANSWERS ON PAGE 232.

GETTING ARTY

ACROSS

1. Big shot in hockey
5. "West Point of the South"
8. Cocktail napkin jotting
12. Act like a couch potato
13. "In one ___ and out the other"
14. "Happy Gilmore" actor Sandler
15. Certain tennis edge
16. Defrosts
18. It features religious symbolism
20. Barbara Bush, ___ Pierce
21. "___ Never Fall in Love Again"
22. BP merger partner
25. Chum
26. Jr. Olympic Games sponsor
29. The oldest known go back 44,000 years
32. 2.95, for Don Drysdale
33. Any top 10 song, say
34. Cause of kitchen tears
35. Comical Olive
36. "How peculiar"
37. It includes street art and any art of today
43. City across the Peace Bridge from Buffalo

44. Body part that may be hazel
45. "Cabaret" star Minnelli
46. Canoe paddle
47. Carpenter's clamp
48. At the crest of
49. "No Such Agency" agcy.
50. **"Jekyll** & Hyde" actress Linda or German river

DOWN

1. Bacon hunk
2. Gaga or Godiva
3. Comedian Ansari
4. Way of showing repentance
5. Classic Chevy, briefly
6. Hawaiian fish, for short
7. From Tehran, say
8. Congested-sounding
9. Floral emanation
10. Far from slack
11. Paramedic, for short
17. Comfortably off
19. Greenhorn
22. 1 or 11, in blackjack
23. Spoil, as a finish
24. Fertility lab supply
25. Area for an orchestra
26. "As Is" singer DiFranco
27. Ages ___ (time long past)

28. Adm.'s outfit
30. Airplane's wing flap
31. Ready to roll, as a car
35. Available for immediate use
36. "Aida" or "Carmen," e.g.
37. San Francisco's ___ Tower

38. Itsy-bitsy pasta
39. Actresses Farrow and Sara
40. Desert descriptor
41. "All ___!" (court command)
42. River of Flanders
43. Cape Canaveral's st.

ANSWERS ON PAGE 233.

CLOTHES AND ACCESSORIES

ACROSS

1. MSNBC rival
4. AWOL chasers
7. Large number
11. Capable of: 2 wds.
12. Chicago trains
13. Pasta that looks like rice
14. Obtained from sheep of the islands: 2 wds.
17. Property claim
18. Intl. commerce group
19. Boxing org.
22. Fuel from the swamp
24. Octoberfest cold one
25. Desirable invitees: 2 wds.
27. Puerto ___, Caribbean island
29. Round fastener
31. Silky fur of the Angora goat
35. Part of the Bible: abbr.
37. Cowboy's mount
38. Prefix for synthetic materials
41. London club district
43. Swindle
44. Schuss downhill
45. Smack
47. Store with men's clothes
52. Pinnacle
53. Again in the music notes
54. Limited choice: 3 wds.
55. Suffer from dehydration
56. "___ luck?"
57. Govt. meteo org.

DOWN

1. Imitations, for short
2. Ultimate degree
3. Winter Holiday song
4. Noisy fight
5. Two-dimensional
6. 9-digit ID
7. Female oink producer
8. Russell ___, Oscar winner
9. Nitrogen, formerly
10. Sorrow
15. First-class
16. Tar
20. ___ ray disc
21. Abbr. in the footnote
23. ___ Burton, director
24. Nonconformist writer
26. Dog command
28. Poisonous berry
30. Turndowns
32. Electric curve
33. World-wide body developing business best practices
34. Tear apart
36. Kurt ___, Nirvana singer

38. "I don't buy it!"
39. Giraffe cousin
40. Defame in writing
42. Brazen girl
46. ___ Penn, actor

48. Office no.
49. AKA, in business
50. Perpendicular to column
51. Century divs.

ANSWERS ON PAGE 233.

HORSE OPERAS

ACROSS

1. Arabian gulf
5. "American ___" (1999 Jason Biggs movie)
8. Architect's design
12. Sioux shelter: Var.
13. Gen.'s counterpart
14. Filigreed
15. On a liner, say
16. Tiny, to Angus
17. About, in contracts
18. 1949 western starring Clayton Moore and Jay Silverheels
21. Cries of discomfort
22. Kind or sort
23. Baseball Hall-of-Famer Tony
26. It's west of Afr.
27. Area for critical patients, briefly
30. 1950s western starring Gregory Peck
33. Alley-___ (basketball play)
34. Beloved animal
35. Grainy, maybe
36. Judge Lance ___ (1995 name in the news)
37. Anderson Cooper's channel
38. 1950 western with James Ellison and Julie Adams
45. "... softly and carry ___ stick"

46. "Texas Tea"
47. Bobber in a harbor
48. Rwanda native
49. It may be heard before a reception
50. Raggedy ___ (some dolls)
51. "Saving Private Ryan" event
52. A pocketful, in rhyme
53. Bee ___ ("Stayin' Alive" group)

DOWN

1. Rat ___ (gun sounds)
2. Act the gossip
3. Fencing weapon
4. "Soul Food" actress
5. Chessboard sixteen
6. Brainstorm, in Paris
7. Honored faculty retirees
8. Shoot at, as bottles on a fence
9. Lana of Smallville
10. Part of an estate
11. Manhattanite, for short
19. Admit
20. Little kid's words after cleaning his plate
23. '60s Pontiac muscle car
24. First of a journalist's five W's
25. Backwoods affirmative
26. At the back of a boat
27. "Addams Family" cousin
28. So-so mark, in school

29. Catering hall vessel
31. Modern film genre with dark themes
32. Purse
36. PC troubleshooter around the office
37. Actress Sevigny
38. Former Saudi king
39. "Nothing beats ___" (old beer slogan)
40. "Come in and ___ spell"
41. In apple-pie order
42. Ancient Germanic character
43. "How steak is done" sauce
44. "Swiss Family Robinson" author Johann

ANSWERS ON PAGE 233.

PARASITE

ACROSS

1. Pitcher plant victim
4. "Parasite" director, producer, and writer: ___ Joon-ho
8. Share some gossip
12. Hawaii's Mauna ___ volcano
13. Flyer to Tel Aviv
14. It means "commander" in Arabic
15. Game lover's purchase
16. Dynamic opener
17. Omar of "House"
18. "Parasite" was Oscar's ___ of 2019
21. Female enlistee in WWII
22. What permissive parents may choose to spare
25. "Faust" character
28. Vets-to-be
29. Number of Disney Dalmatians
30. Pizza joint appliance
31. Party with power
32. Give a long look
33. Beyond the horizon
34. And the rest, briefly
35. Where van Gogh painted "The Night Cafe"

36. Philadelphia hockey team
38. New Deal agcy. of 1933
39. "Parasite" won four major Oscars, including one for "Best International ___"
44. Ump's ruling
46. Campsite visitor
47. Take-home item
48. Type of bond, for short
49. Slangy turnarounds
50. Colony member
51. Arcade game ___-Ball
52. State of comfort
53. Dit's counterpart in Morse code

DOWN

1. Toning target
2. Wolf's gait
3. Barks sharply
4. "Help me out here, bud"
5. Olive oil's ___ acid
6. Sting figure
7. Opening between the vocal cords
8. Big name in tractors and such
9. Bygone Chrysler
10. Drink sample
11. Slugger's stat
19. Sealy choice

20. Nervous speaker's sounds
23. Leak out slowly
24. Breaks down
25. Tip, as one's derby
26. Feedback for a prof.
27. Nearly mint, to a collector
28. Big chain in health supplements
31. "I'm not making it up!"
32. Rival of Seles

34. The Mesozoic, e.g.
35. Reluctant
37. Causing chills, maybe
38. They beat twos
40. Iris container
41. Apple store purchase
42. Clark's crush
43. Legend
44. Most NPR stations
45. Puffin, e.g.

1	2	3		4	5	6	7		8	9	10	11
12				13					14			
15				16					17			
18			19					20				
		21				22				23	24	
25	26	27			28				29			
30				31				32				
33			34				35					
36		37				38						
	39				40				41	42	43	
44	45			46					47			
48				49					50			
51				52					53			

ANSWERS ON PAGE 233.

GRANDMA'S PANTRY

ACROSS

1. Leveling wedge
5. Copy of a mag.
8. Big ___
12. Animal rights org.
13. Reggae relative
14. Dutch treat
15. Strong plow pullers
16. See-through data: abbr.
17. Sand hill
18. Orange spread
21. Indian holiday destination
22. ___ Brynner, actor
24. Multi ___, like cut gems
28. Excite: 2 wds.
31. Computer port
32. Abner's radio friend
34. Go astray
35. Place: Latin
38. Pulpy refuse in sugar-making
41. Resume, for short
43. Ammo unit: abbr.
45. Candied fruit
48. Greek portico
50. US secretive org.
51. Boost: abbr.
53. Estonian or Latvian
54. Architects' org.
55. Arm of the Black Sea
56. Loony
57. ''Bad'' cholesterol
58. Musical mark

DOWN

1. Sugar quantity in recipes
2. Witch's curse
3. News bit
4. Cope
5. "Moby-Dick" narrator
6. Gull-like bird
7. Unfortunately
8. Interfere
9. Musical direction
10. ___-of-war, battleship
11. Final word
19. Decompose
20. Arctic diver
23. Dogcatcher's cargo
25. Starting from: 2 wds.
26. North-of-the-border network
27. Nickname
29. Cry of success
30. Can for future use
33. ___ law
36. Nazi submarines: 2 wds.
37. One of the sixty in an h.
39. Safari sight
40. Rocky's Balboa love
42. Garbage
44. Book ID: abbr.
45. Wild West revolver

46. Bibliographical abbr.
47. ___ Ferrari, auto designer

49. Kind of cross
52. Simple sack

ANSWERS ON PAGE 234.

FINISH THE ADAGE

ACROSS

1. After-school group
5. "Cakes and ___" (Maugham novel)
8. Didn't have to guess
12. Aesop character who lost a race
13. ___ Fail (Irish "Stone of Destiny")
14. Actress Petty of "Orange Is the New Black"
15. One in agreement
17. "Bearded" flower
18. Practice . . . (finish the adage)
20. Fleur de ___
21. Big palooka
22. Chick of jazz
25. Au ___ (in gravy)
26. Big name in casual clothes
29. Good fences make . . . (finish the adage)
32. Charged-up particle
33. Airline to Amsterdam
34. Breakwater
35. "Get it?"
36. "How delightful!"
37. A watched . . . (finish the adage)
44. Peru's capital
45. Invites for a visit

46. Colorado Springs Acad.
47. "___-Pan" (Clavell novel)
48. Air outlet
49. Diner's list
50. German "one"
51. It is, in Spain

DOWN

1. Ballplayer's cheekful
2. Eye protector
3. "Major" constellation
4. Describing a brow
5. Glee club voices
6. "In ___ of flowers . . ."
7. One of a swimmer's pair
8. Film studio light
9. "The Thin Man" role
10. "Spamalot" creator Idle
11. Coin-in-the-fountain thought
16. Joltin' Joe, e.g.
19. They have to be done fast
22. 3-D graphics in movies
23. Tic-tac-toe win
24. Harry Potter's pal Weasley
25. Carrey or Belushi
26. "You've ___ Mail"
27. It's often left hanging

28. "Gangnam Style" rapper
30. Kick up a notch
31. Make sense for
35. Military slang for a muddled mess
36. Big name in pest control
37. "Clue" professor
38. River from Belgium to France
39. Fraud-fighting Fed
40. Morales of "Bad Boys"
41. "Blue Tail Fly" singer Burl
42. Fasting period
43. Latina lass: Abbr.

BADDIES OF FICTION

ACROSS

1. Hot rocks
5. Boggy land
8. Belch, say
12. "Deliver us from ___"
13. "Do the Right Thing" director
14. Hip-hop trio Salt-N-___
15. Count calories
16. Archer's wood
17. Arrogant sort
18. "The Demon Barber of Fleet Street"
21. 1985 Kurosawa classic
22. A in German class?
23. Coal worker
26. "The Big Bang Theory" character from India
27. Barrel at a bash
30. "Nightmare on Elm Street" villain
33. It's often left hanging
34. A pal of Pooh
35. Easy gait
36. Big embrace
37. "Fifth Beatle" Yoko
38. "Psycho" weirdo
43. Sonny or Chastity
44. "___ culpa"
45. "Don't worry about me"
47. Orders a dog to attack
48. Escort's offering
49. 1980s Dodge model

50. "Iliad" war god
51. "___ Skylark" (Shelley)
52. Apollo acronym

DOWN

1. Blazed a trail
2. Alamo alternative
3. Panoramic sight
4. Did a tailoring job
5. Robin Hood portrayer Errol
6. Bigfoot's shoe size?
7. It begins in January
8. Big name in printers
9. Fix, as socks
10. It can help you carry a tune
11. Eatery check
19. Body part that vibrates
20. Baja border city
23. Artist's degree
24. Abbr. on a clothing reject tag
25. Hoop hanger
26. "King Kong" and "Citizen Kane" studio
27. C.I.A.'s Soviet counterpart
28. Aquarium wriggler
29. College sr.'s exam
31. Something to meditate on
32. Feeling

36. 1990s candidate ___ Perot
37. 2009 Peace Prize Nobelist
38. "Film ___" (dark movie genre)
39. "The Raven" start

40. "Fiddling" emperor
41. Madame Bovary
42. Heirs, often
43. "Be prepared" org.
46. Cadenza maker

 ANSWERS ON PAGE 234.

SORRY

ACROSS

1. With 12-Across, "Sorry!"
5. Ticket remnant
8. Proportionately
9. Rock beater, in a game
10. Sit in on, as a class
12. See 1-Across
14. Bottom line
15. Sorry!
17. Home of the slender-waisted
18. Party manager, in Congress
21. With 24-Across, sorry
22. Vacation, for short
23. 140 characters or less
24. See 21-Across

DOWN

1. Weeping
2. Canon camera
3. You may get a rise out of it
4. Consume entirely
6. Pudding ingredient
7. Sound in a dog pound
9. "Saturday Night Live" bit
11. It vends odds and ends
13. Kids' jumping game
15. Employer's enticement
16. Chronic loser
17. Isle mentioned in "When I'm Sixty-Four"
19. Vietnam capital
20. Mild complaint

ANSWERS ON PAGE 234.

DRIVING AROUND

ACROSS

1. Back-talking
8. Went for a rebound, say
13. "Same here"
14. Hyper
15. Most dubious
16. Plant equivalent of blood vessels
17. Shoe-size letters
18. "Forbidden" perfume
20. Passing try, in football stats
21. Amusement park vehicle
24. Three-R's org.
25. Lee Greenwood's "God Bless the ___"
26. Nervous or solar ___
28. Bat an eyelash, say
31. Greenish-blue shades
32. Like royal descent, usually
34. Camera shot
35. Ex of Mickey, Artie, and Frank
36. Musical symbol
41. Annual Asian holiday
42. Change one's story?
43. To be, with you
44. ___ acid (mild antiseptic)
46. Missing something

49. "___ Gay" (famous B-29)
50. Anti
51. Stave off
52. Prairie homes

DOWN

1. It's rarely a hit
2. Farewell, to Francoise
3. Command to Fido
4. Star Wars initials
5. Suffix with social or suburban
6. Cosa ___
7. Scored a "gentleman's grade"
8. Lincoln or Infiniti, e.g.
9. Tarzan player Ron
10. Peach Bowl site
11. Like a 12-year-old
12. Large orchestral gongs
19. Humanities degs.
22. Faultless
23. What the British call a station wagon
27. In ___ (on the same page)
28. Tow truck type
29. Easy mark
30. Racing, as pacers
33. Set the pace
34. Thick, creamy soup
37. Bite lightly, as a puppy might

60

38. "I Believe" singer Frankie

39. Wipe away, as chalk

40. Some hat materials

45. Land in the Seine

47. Music's Carly ___ Jepsen

48. Gratuity

ANSWERS ON PAGE 235.

DAVID O. RUSSELL MOVIES

ACROSS

1. Biblical hymn
6. 1966 song that asked "What's it all about?"
11. Biggest human bone
12. Jury members, supposedly
13. Former Army post in Calif.
14. Not very interesting
15. 1999 satirical war drama directed by David O. Russell
17. Evil spirits
18. Fats, to a nutritionist
21. A musing sound
24. Makes by working
25. Tree branch, in a lullaby
27. Big word on a buck
28. Actor Robert ___ has appeared in three David O. Russell films
29. Dressy neckwear
32. 2010 sports drama directed by David O. Russell
36. Support beam
37. Sailor's shore time
38. Impolite looker
39. Icelandic tales
40. "Big Three" meeting site of 1945
41. Particular angle

DOWN

1. Fizzled-out firecracker sound
2. MacFarlane of "Family Guy"
3. Cupid alias
4. Baited
5. 2002 title role for Adam Sandler
6. Difficult high school sci. course
7. Country star Rimes
8. Chinese decorating philosophy
9. Nest eggs, for short
10. Class for U.S. immigrants: Abbr.
16. Canadian rd. distances
18. Melissa ___ won a Best Supporting Actress Oscar for 32-Across
19. "Dr. No" novelist Fleming
20. Prepare a new wine for drinking
22. Baseball boss: Abbr.
23. Electrical unit now called a siemens
25. Dogs like Snoopy
26. Hush-hush, slangily
28. 506, in old Rome
30. Bowler's start-over button

31. SAG-___ (actors' union)
32. "Animal House" wear
33. "And there you have it!"
34. Fashion's ___-Picone

35. Staycation goal
36. 2015 comedy-drama directed by David O. Russell

ANSWERS ON PAGE 235.

OLD PRINTING HOUSE

ACROSS

1. Golf hazard
5. Historic beginning
8. Taj Mahal site
12. Hindu attire
13. Fronted
14. Spring bloom
15. One of the Big Four accounting firms
16. Black cuckoo
17. Hose issue
18. Setting material into a form to be used in printing
22. ___ Park, IL
24. Landlocked republic in central Africa: var.
27. Housetop worker
30. Sixth sense: abbr.
31. Floral garland
32. Monetary subunit of the baht (in Thailand)
36. By agreed order: 2 wds.
39. Blood clots
41. Essential in producing daily newspaper: 3 wds.
45. Latvian capital
46. Versatile vehicle, for short
47. Pre-weekend shout: abbr.
49. March 15th

50. D.C. bigwig
51. Lothario's look
52. Rendezvous
53. Epilogue
54. Studied

DOWN

1. Sound of reproach
2. Spellbound
3. Organised fighting force
4. Dirty place
5. Kind of TV screen
6. Extend
7. Magazine employee
8. Japanese martial art
9. Smile broadly
10. Boxing space
11. Query
19. Antiquity, old-style
20. Excessively
21. Newspapers
23. Make email touchable
25. Stars and Stripes land: abbr.
26. Fitting
28. Seasonal ___
29. Sonnet ending
33. After much delay: 2 wds.
34. Stanley Cup org.
35. Grumble
36. Threaten to occur
37. Chicago Bulls' org.

38. Walk quietly
40. As a rule
41. Hitchhike
42. Double curve

43. Like rich batter
44. Stir up
45. Canyon feature
48. Satiated

ANSWERS ON PAGE 235.

YOU WANNA PIECE O' ME?

ACROSS

1. Blow up
9. Cups and saucers
10. Bug-eating plant
11. Listen
14. Stop fasting
15. Electronics whiz
17. Race to the _____
20. Gal's counterpart
21. Assist
23. Takes a closer look
25. Stale and then some
26. Tender help to a walker

DOWN

2. Hunter in the night sky
3. Historic period
4. Not in harmony
5. Energy beam
6. From the heart
7. Train station
8. Carve out of rock
12. Getting rid of
13. Title role for Valerie Harper
16. Give a false alarm
18. Lived off very little money
19. "Just the same . . ."
20. Thingamajig
22. Knot tying site
24. John or McCartney
25. Fireside chat pres.

ANSWERS ON PAGE 235.

TO KILL A MOCKINGBIRD

ACROSS

1. "To Kill a Mockingbird"'s state
8. Ancient Greek gathering place
13. Oil and ___
14. Painter of cafe scenes
15. "College" member who votes for president
16. ___ once (suddenly)
17. "___ Lama Ding Dong" ('60s tune)
18. Golda Meir was one
20. "Mockingbird" girl and narrator
22. "Mockingbird" character Radley
23. Control-tower employee: Abbr.
24. As of yet
26. Coin of little worth
27. "The Great" czar
30. Gravelly ridges
33. 1921 man-vs.-robot play
34. "Grey's Anatomy" role
36. A pitching ace has a low one, in brief
37. Outer: Prefix
38. Once ___ (annually)
42. Asked someone to "hush"
44. Mechanical click
45. Go for ___ (take the car out)
46. Like wanted criminals
49. Cotton thread used for gloves
50. Christmas tree shedding
51. Asian coins or weights
52. Goldilocks's pride

DOWN

1. Affirms with confidence
2. Delicate purple
3. Prefix meaning "wind"
4. "___ I said so!"
5. 15-percenter: Abbr.
6. "Little Red Book" chairman
7. Exuberant Spanish cry
8. Ruben ___, Phillies Gold Glove-winning shortstop
9. Big, fancy dinner
10. How some cars are acquired
11. House broker
12. Gregory's role in "Mockingbird"
19. More achy
21. Craggy hill
25. Atticus, Scout and Jem's last name
27. Make ready for a winter storm, as a highway

28. Continent-spanning landmass
29. Roam (about)
31. Assigner of nine-digit nos.
32. Data-input devices
35. Former Secretary General of the U.N.
37. Anglo-Saxon serfs
39. British nobles

40. "Oh, shucks!"
41. Like May-to-August months
43. Best friend of Jem and Scout in "Mockingbird"
47. Dutch artist Gerard ___ Borch
48. "Mockingbird" author Harper ___

ANSWERS ON PAGE 236.

YOGA CLASS

ACROSS

1. Bro
5. Small batteries
8. "Dilbert" character
12. Windows alternative
13. Low grade
14. Level, in Britain
15. And so on
17. Fashion magazine
18. Way of sitting in yoga: 2 wds.
20. "___ so fast!"
21. 1975 Wimbledon champ
22. Diplomat's talent
25. Quality of being flexible
28. ___ Gardner, actress
29. Highlanders, e.g.
31. Third letter
32. Way of bearing one's body
34. City on the Rhone
35. Distinctive atmosphere
36. Russian river
38. Complete attention
44. In a frenzy
45. Opening prayer on the eve of Yom Kippur: 2 wds.
46. Menu option
47. Japanese vegetable
48. Scorch
49. Med. school class

50. ___ a balloon
51. Better ___

DOWN

1. Sword fight
2. Golden rule word
3. Wordsmith's ref.
4. Shakespeare stage direction
5. Highly skilled
6. Dynamic prefix
7. White condiment from the ocean: 2 wds.
8. ___ Franklin, singer
9. Prominence: var.
10. Norway's capital
11. Eager
16. General on a Chinese menu
19. Egyptian goddess
22. Designate
23. Macao coin
24. Famous Venetian lover
25. "The Black Cat" author
26. Corp. top dog
27. Japanese currency
29. "No problem"
30. Get started: 2 wds.
33. Fanfare on a trumpet
34. Somewhat behind
36. Lowest deck on a ship
37. Topeka's loc.
38. House in Havana
39. Gulf state

70

40. List of tasks header:
2 wds.
41. Creative spark

42. Not written
43. It's a blaster

ANSWERS ON PAGE 236.

PHILHARMONIC

ACROSS

1. The basics
5. Pat lightly
8. Funny internet depiction
12. Brazil's neighbor
13. Smart TV remote button
14. ___ Office
15. First public performance
17. Breathing sound
18. Old train engine driving force
19. Kind of ancient column
20. Taxi
22. Former auto make
23. Company exec responsible for brand management
26. Von Karajan or Mehta, e.g.
31. University mil. group
33. Neb. neighbor
34. Greek liqueur
35. Instrumentalists in philharmonic
38. Keyboard key
39. Lincoln nickname
40. Heart monitor: abbr.
42. Prepare for surgery
46. Gloomy
50. ___ Baldwin, actor
51. Complex music composition
53. Missing
54. 25th letter
55. Beginner: var.
56. Suffix with comment
57. Fairy queen
58. Mil. school

DOWN

1. Run on smartphones, for short
2. "Sesame Street" character
3. Native Canadian
4. Poisonous small tree
5. Dr. ___, rapper
6. Unsubstantial
7. Early date identifier
8. Algeria's neighbor
9. ___ Hunter, novelist
10. Saharan country
11. Util. bill
16. Apple computer
19. Luau cooking pit
21. Haul with a tackle
22. Esteem to the extreme
23. ___-Magnon man
24. Casablanca's country: abbr.
25. Non-Rx: abbr.
27. Big Apple newsp.
28. Wed. preceder
29. Parts of lbs.

30. Mythical bird
32. "Canterbury Tales" author
36. Flow back
37. Electrical letters
41. ___ Garbo, actress
42. Heroic tale
43. Congeal

44. Gambling mecca
45. Spanish painter
47. ___ Clapton, guitarist
48. Big name in shaving
49. Crucifix
51. Moutain basin
52. Pen point

ANSWERS ON PAGE 236.

FICTIONAL PLACES

ACROSS

1. Computer port
4. "Sonic the Hedgehog" developer
8. Apartment in London
12. "America the Beautiful" closer
13. Aspirin, e.g.
14. Candy in a cylindrical package
15. Dry red wine
17. "Beetle Bailey" dog
18. Exotic jelly fruit
19. Like a clay pot
21. Home of Queen Eliz.
23. Boardroom graphic
24. "Lost Horizon" paradise
29. Rock's ___ Speedwagon
30. Drawn tight
31. Caviar, literally
32. Treasure site in "It's a Mad, Mad, Mad, Mad World"
33. 9-1-1 responder
34. Musical's mystical village
36. Far from poetic
38. Big Columbus sch.
39. Egyptian monarch who abdicated in 1952
42. Eniwetok first
46. Anita of jazz fame
47. Wolf in sheep's clothing, e.g.

49. Costa follower
50. Glide like a buzzard
51. It may be positively charged
52. Bambi's aunts
53. Actress Ione
54. ___-Caps (Nestle candy)

DOWN

1. Govt. shore patrol
2. 12-time Pro Bowl player Junior
3. Ali of "Arabian Nights"
4. Leapt suddenly
5. "Ich Bin ___ Berliner": JFK
6. Fox program about a choir
7. Rival of Aspen
8. Foamy cover
9. Fictional ladies' man
10. Bruce Banner, to the Hulk
11. Fictional city in "Who Framed Roger Rabbit?" (1988)
16. Gala or ball
20. "His Master's Voice" record label
22. Angry dog's warning
24. Fictional town with robotic wives
25. Amateur broadcaster's gear
26. Event for Foyt
27. Dalmatian number
28. Big brand of blocks

74

32. Buffalo Wild Wings nickname based on its initials

34. Mitt Romney's alma mater, for short

35. How some shells are washed

37. Tofu beans

40. Barely touch, on a pool table

41. "Fine here"

43. "(Sittin' on) the Dock of the Bay" singer Redding

44. 12 men have walked on it

45. Capital of Moravia

48. Wages

ANSWERS ON PAGE 236.

GODS OF THE OCEANS

ACROSS

1. God of the sea
7. Braid
11. Variant of an original recording
12. Headstone inscription
13. Glance
15. Dagger marks in old manuscripts
17. Metal ring supporting a net in basketball
18. Footnote word
20. Young fellow
21. Weighed to determine a tare
23. Prescriptions
24. Chemical suffix
25. Draw new borders
27. Barbie's boyfriend
28. Express in words
31. Scope or range
34. King: French
35. Mosaic layer
37. Web address ending
38. Quagmire
39. Finger or toe
43. Label in a tweet
44. Rainbows
46. Thomas ___, composer
47. "Silas Marner" author
49. Pipe for conveying air: 2 wds.
51. Just out

52. Struck down
53. Standard deviation letter
54. Daughter of Agamemnon

DOWN

1. Period spent sleeping
2. Earlier in time
3. Egg-based painter's medium
4. Strike caller
5. Not yet final, in law
6. Outdoor sit in stone
7. Formal high school balls
8. Ad-___ (improvise)
9. Dumb and hulking
10. Spear with three prongs
14. Mauna ___
16. Burdened
19. Kick out
22. ___ Moines, Iowa capital
26. Taxi ticker
28. Shapeshifting god who served Poseidon
29. Hourly
30. Ship's ropes
32. Crossed out
33. Like common chords
36. If there happens to be need

38. Muslim decree
40. Low-ranking soldier
41. Company name ender: abbr.
42. Fish in a tank

45. Window ledge
48. Lower priced software product keys
50. Charlotte ___, actress

ANSWERS ON PAGE 237.

ONCE UPON A TIME…IN HOLLYWOOD

ACROSS

1. Soft drink choice
5. Life force in Chinese philosophy
8. More than willing
12. Like some cheeses and wines
13. Solo of space opera
14. Bone up quickly
15. He plays Cliff Booth, Rick Dalton's stunt double, in "Once Upon a Time…in Hollywood"
17. Incur a bleep
18. Alum-to-be
19. Vote in
21. Crisp quality
22. Element of one's inheritance
23. Sing your own praises
26. Apple Records founders
29. "u r hilarious!"
30. Blue cartoon critter
32. Verb ending in old verse
33. Knocks over
35. Officially give up
36. Song from "Carmen," say
37. Fundraising sch. group
39. Boric and citric
40. Ill will
44. Like long chances

45. ___ DiCaprio plays actor Rick Dalton in the Tinseltown hit
47. Sicily's tallest mountain
48. Newcomer's study: abbr.
49. She kills Jabba the Hutt
50. Warm winter wear
51. Holy jurisdiction
52. E-mail screen button

DOWN

1. Some red wines, casually
2. Fairy-tale meanie
3. With less fat
4. Abacus activity
5. Cricket call
6. Beanie or beret
7. 98, but not **98.**6
8. Southern drawl, e.g.
9. Martial arts legend played by Mike Moh in "Once Upon a Time…in Hollywood"
10. Bottom position
11. Ammonium has three
16. Island finger food
20. Foliage element
23. Diner sandwich inits.
24. Pouch-dwelling Pooh pal
25. He plays casting agent Marvin Schwarz in "Once Upon a Time…in Hollywood"
26. Airport shuttle

78

27. Airport gate posting, for short

28. Pronoun for any vessel

30. Hit a slick spot

31. Children's malady, often

34. Like some screams or urges

35. Gondola routes

37. Blue-collar worker

38. Loafer color

39. Member of the chorus

41. Canadian native

42. Viking god

43. It's between the shoulders

44. Put on a button, say

46. Tampa-to-Miami dir.

ANSWERS ON PAGE 237.

MEDICAL RESEARCH

ACROSS

1. Max ___, boxer
5. Forcibly put to sleep
8. Material
12. ___ Thompson, actress
13. Afghani coin
14. Lhasa ___, breed of dog
15. Slightly: 2 wds.
16. Indonesian island group
17. Cover the inner side of the roof
18. Obtained from infected individuals: 2 wds.
21. Pond protozoans
23. Muslim woman of high rank in Pakistan
27. Narrow groove
30. Drug safety test: 2 wds.
31. Scoop up, as salsa with a chip
32. Protection
33. Knight's cloak
37. Branch of science dealing with microscopic forms of life
43. Car with a bar
44. Hobo
45. ___ Guthrie, singer
46. Collections of anecdotes

47. British verb ending
48. Ship part
49. Corp. Leadership
50. FedEx rival
51. Car horn sound

DOWN

1. Wally's TV brother, with "the"
2. Both: Prefix
3. Mideast potentate
4. Pro ___ (proportionally)
5. Paroxysm
6. Surrounding radiant lights
7. Exactly vertical
8. Melted cheese served with potatoes
9. Olympics blade
10. Sale condition
11. Joke response: abbr.
19. Layered
20. Attacking thrust in fencing
22. Shoreline indentations
23. A followers
24. ___ Lilly & Co
25. Turn the pig upside down
26. Price per piece: 2 wds.
28. Persian floor covering
29. ___ Amin, Ugandan dictator

34. Hollow-horned ruminants
35. Embarrass
36. Star in Orion
37. Chinese dynasty
38. Mosque VIP

39. 100,000 in India
40. Black&white treat
41. Secluded valley
42. Central egg part
43. Hasty escape

13-LETTER WORDS

ACROSS

1. Dog, cat or hamster
4. Baby sheep
8. Certain hotel amenity
12. "4," sometimes: abbr.
13. Actor Morales
14. " ___ and the King of Siam"
15. "Blame It On ___" (Caine movie)
16. 75 percent, say
17. "Diga Diga Doo" trio
18. Professional needler?
21. It sounds like "air"
22. Fair way to divide things
23. Ages, as tobacco
26. Bikini half
27. All-even score
28. "Author unknown": Abbr.
29. "Anthem" author Rand
30. Prefix meaning "ten"
31. Bull Run soldier
32. Aspiring Ph.D.'s test
33. Less dotty
34. For the time being, in Latin
36. Former "Buffy the Vampire Slayer" network
37. Bird-watcher
42. Currency unit in Iran
43. Sign of a skunk
44. Big name in video games
45. Anchored fastener
46. Place where salt is found
47. "___ be my pleasure!"
48. Bilko and Snorkel
49. Startled squeals
50. "Born as"

DOWN

1. Legal assistant, for short
2. "Aeneid" or "Iliad"
3. Bad thing to drop in public
4. Wide-eyed primates of Madagascar
5. In concert
6. Opposite of fem.
7. Heron relative
8. "M*A*S*H" chaplain
9. Certain long odds
10. Common pizzeria order
11. Just over 12 months ago
19. Back end of a hammer
20. Cavaliers' sch.
23. Sedan shelters
24. Consistently accurate
25. Johnson Space Center humanoid project
26. Terse ta-ta

29. Sleeve feature
30. "Rats!"
32. See the point of
33. Combination utensils
35. Pinball no-nos
36. Horseshoe-shaped bike protector

38. "Garfield" beagle
39. "Bingo!"
40. .com location
41. Wave maker

ANSWERS ON PAGE 237.

OLD VIDEO GAMES

ACROSS

1. Old video game container
8. Shade of blue
11. Loving murmur
12. Defendants, in law
13. Compass dir.
14. Catches
16. Boolean logic operator
17. Contents of some bags
18. Kidney ezyme
19. Even more intense
21. Outfit
23. Most of Libya
27. Jacob's Twin
31. 1978 arcade classic from Japan: 2 wds.
34. Elusive furry creature
35. Anterior wings in beetles
36. Solid lump of gold
40. Knight's squire
43. Improvised: 2 wds.
47. Maiden name preceder
48. Typist injury: abbr.
49. Christopher ___, actor
50. Blast maker
51. Doctrine
52. Before, in poems
53. Aiport posting: abbr.
54. Atari rival in the 90's (as in home computers manufacturing)

DOWN

2. Field measure
3. Reddish-brown
4. Pith helmet
5. Blueprint
6. Spirits in a bottle
7. Pillow filler
8. UFO-tracking org.
9. Midleg
10. Wine label info
14. Having long locks
15. Entangle
20. Slender
22. ___ chi, Chinese excercise
24. Big goon
25. Sombrero, e.g.
26. Small drupes making up a fruit like a blackberry
28. Match part
29. Opposite of dep.
30. Grace period
32. Victory sign
33. Sacrifice site
37. Finno-___ (language group)
38. Painter's plaster
39. Fairy stories brother
40. Initial stake
41. Landlord's due
42. Current ___ (as in a esports)

84

44. Owner's acquisition
45. Medal recipient
46. Concluded

ANSWERS ON PAGE 238.

BUILDING SITE

ACROSS

1. Clark ___, movie star
6. Time delay
9. Dance company: abbr.
12. Position
13. UN workers' org.
14. "___ won't!": 2 wds.
15. Florida resort
16. Possible word
17. Prince, to a king
18. Manufacture for rapid assembling on the building site
22. State of perplexity
23. Pro football grp.
26. ___ anglais (horn)
27. Ancient aromatic ointment
31. Thoroughfare
33. Frightening sort
35. Greek salad ingredient
36. IRS forms producer: abbr.
37. Govt. Property overseer
38. Golden Gate Bridge paint: 2 wds.
42. Act of building
47. Vietnamese coin
48. ___ polloi
49. Coastal feature
51. BBC rival
52. Distant but within sight
53. Money of Nigeria
54. Arabic letter
55. Camper fuel: abbr.
56. Marriage ceremony VIP

DOWN

1. Wireless network standard: abbr.
2. Expectantly
3. Grizzly
4. Crippled
5. Skyscraper, e.g.
6. Capable of bending freely
7. Theft preventer
8. Gentiles
9. Vase looped handle
10. Start a computer
11. Pitchfork part
19. Heaps: 2 wds.
20. Biblical miracle site
21. Well-known audiotape brand, once
24. Unit of workload of an employed person: abbr.
25. Old computer screen: abbr.
28. Leo Messi's homeland: abbr.
29. Hi-___ monitor
30. Mild swear word
32. Listening devices
33. Work detail
34. Thin layer
36. Bonding with adhesive

39. Kind of alcohol
40. Hang loosely
41. Iran currency
42. Marker
43. Pledge

44. Stellar phenomenon
45. Mishmash
46. Roman emperor and arsonist
50. Topper

ANSWERS ON PAGE 238.

BLUE BLOODS

ACROSS

1. A bit damp
6. Hook or Cook: Abbr.
10. Split apart
11. Take on, as employees
12. Movie trailer exhortation
13. "... lovin' the spin ___"
14. He's Police Commissioner Frank Reagan
16. Grinning emoticons
17. Agent Gold of "Entourage"
20. Brand on many an auto racer's jacket
21. Young chaps
23. "Dinner at ___"
27. Danny Reagan's wife who was killed in a helicopter crash
29. Paintball impact sound
30. Lively tune
31. Org. that owns WorldSeries.com
33. "Hollywood Squares" symbols
34. It beats an ace
38. She's feisty Officer "Eddie" Janko, Jamie Reagan's fiancée
42. Jewish calendar's twelfth month

43. Cliched
44. Gold cloth
45. Affix a new price to
46. Arrived feet-first
47. Ape from Borneo, briefly

DOWN

1. "Gorillas in the ___," 1988 film
2. "___'Clock Jump" (Basie theme)
3. Couple in a gossip column
4. "The ___ Family Robinson"
5. Aboriginal emblems
6. Metaphorical prescription for one in a tizzy
7. "A Man and a Woman" actress
8. Big-ticket
9. Distance races
15. About a quarter of a gallon
17. Cry said with a sigh
18. Expressway exit
19. Charming scene
22. Played tag, e.g.
24. E.U. group
25. Pail problem
26. Blows up with explosives

28. Trip planner's aid
32. Chic eatery
34. Egg outlines
35. Tennis champ Rafael
36. As a friend, in France

37. More desirable to collectors
39. "Lovely ___" (Beatles song)
40. ___ angle (obliquely)
41. B-movie baddie

SCARY MONSTERS

ACROSS

1. Cathedral city in north France
8. Scratch
12. Verdant
13. Web access enabler: abbr.
14. Fine-tune
15. ___ von Bismarck
16. "All Things Considered" network
17. Tiny screen symbol
18. Largest of the Marianas
19. ___ Scala, actress
20. Confab
21. Imaginary monster
24. Terrier's bark
27. Hard wood pin
28. Get rid of
31. Sorrowful through deprivation
33. Rubbishy
34. Steeple
35. Put to the test
36. NYSE unit
37. Grotesquely carved figure
40. Scrooge utterances
42. Stiff bristle
43. Impudence
47. Low female choir voices
48. Fannie ___

49. Threesome
50. "Tres ___!"
51. Miss after marriage
52. Nobleman
53. Warbled
54. Accumulated on the surface

DOWN

1. Wooden soles footwear
2. Tutsi mortal enemies
3. Dog star
4. Diamond shape
5. Malaysian money
6. Spotted
7. Waterfall effect
8. Bustling Great Lakes port
9. Scottish lake with legendary serpent
10. Indonesian ox
11. Left
22. Proposal
23. ___ Streep, actress
24. Washboard ___
25. Weightlifting unit
26. Cause fear in
29. Cryptographic network protocol: abbr.
30. Norse war god
32. Removing from existence
33. Abstinence
35. In the direction of

38. Dangerous rays
39. Organic compound
40. Streisand, in headlines
41. Inter ___

44. Oman native
45. King's title
46. Convinced

ANSWERS ON PAGE 238.

GAS STATION

ACROSS

1. Acidity measures
4. Providers obligations: abbr.
7. Knucklehead
10. Can't stand
12. Beloved
13. ___-di-dah
14. Trojan War hero
15. Give or take
16. Bio stat
17. Air pump figure
20. USSR succesor
21. "___ the land of the free …"
22. "Monty Python" network
25. Cat's cry
27. Right away: abbr.
31. Car coolant or antifreeze
35. Deep male voice
36. Chinese dynasty
37. Tolkien's forest dweller
38. Silent OK
41. Degree from MIT
43. Does not run on rails: 2 wds.
49. Sailor
50. Moved ultra fast
51. Old Asian weight measure
52. Pair

53. Strange
54. Protomatter
55. Capital of Panama?
56. Harmful pesticide
57. Cook in oil

DOWN

1. Excellent, slangily
2. Mecca visitor
3. Celeb
4. Sahara quality
5. Cattle catcher
6. Originated
7. Controversial orchard spray
8. Wise wizard
9. Any ship
11. Board operative
12. County in southwestern England
18. Southern Arizona Indian
19. Eurasia mountains
22. "Hang on a sec" online
23. Meadow sound
24. LP successors
26. Thrill
28. Take to court
29. Discomfort
30. Computer file standard for print
32. "___ it weird?"
33. Treatment
34. Many in school

39. Marveled aloud
40. ___ fruits
42. Not countryside
43. Grimace
44. Woodwind instrument
45. Ramp for skateborders
46. Young whale

47. Odd look
48. Abounding with Massachusetts state trees
49. Annual macroeconomic stat

ANSWERS ON PAGE 239.

GONE FISHIN'

ACROSS

1. Catch for a grizzly
7. Largest mammals
13. "Have a sample!"
14. Repetitive way to learn
15. Desdemona's love, in opera
16. Litter holder
17. London theater district
19. 6-point football scores
20. Auto supplier for the Swedish royal family
21. Aquarium favorite
24. Conger's catch
27. Sheriff-badge shape
29. Big bosses
30. Brilliantly colored flower
32. Oak tree wannabes
34. Backyard tree dangler
35. Abrasive soap brand
37. Posed for pix
38. In the cereal bowl too long, maybe
40. Business letter addressees
42. "Mer" makeup
43. Processor created by Apple, IBM and Motorola
47. Cuba's Fidel or Raul
50. ___ Beach (California resort)
51. First stages
52. Joe Lieberman's middle name
53. Recess rebuttal, perhaps
54. Cocktail crustacean

DOWN

1. Do pier work
2. Comedian Johnson of "Laugh-In"
3. Caustics in soaps
4. Casts off the skin
5. Like some condos
6. Hospital unit for newborns
7. Pugilism org.
8. Hilton rival
9. Chrysler Building's style
10. Maine delicacies
11. Area commanded by DDE
12. Gender
18. Alias, for a co.
22. "Mazes and Monsters" writer Jaffe
23. 2nd in charge
24. Beanery sign
25. Basso Pinza of "South Pacific"
26. Generosity
28. Stuffed Italian pockets
31. Papal envoys

94

33. Something to roll up your windows for
36. "Little Orphan Annie" bodyguard with "the"
39. Mongolian tents
41. "Popeye" creator
44. Fashion designer Gernreich

45. ___ Penh, Cambodia's capital (variant)
46. Complain about a fish dinner?
47. Boston trademark
48. Munich : Jahr :: Madrid : ___
49. Baja bear

 ANSWERS ON PAGE 239.

IN THE DOJO

ACROSS

1. Andean wood sorrel
4. Fabricated
8. Gush forth
12. One of the ISPs
13. Samoan city
14. Slippery trees
15. Thrown punch
17. Adult content: abbr.
18. Three-toed sloth
19. Sweden-based airline
21. Finnish steam bath
25. Respond
29. Helpful tip
30. Spanish lace scarf
32. Combine
33. Old French monetary unit
34. ___ Cruise, actor
35. Blood cancer
37. Fake
38. Halloween choice
39. Insane
40. Fish eggs
42. Akkadian god
43. Big name in imaging, once
46. Perpendicular leg strike: 2 wds.
51. Leave out
52. Kadett maker
53. Sorority letter
54. ___ Bryant, NBA legend
55. Blog piece
56. Youngster

DOWN

1. Fed. budget agency
2. Civil War side: abbr.
3. Mandela's party
4. Crime syndicate
5. Egyptian sacred bull
6. Bad-mouth, in slang
7. Dines
8. Teacher in dojo
9. Polite request word: abbr.
10. Voltage meas.
11. Compass dir.
16. Immanuel ___, philosopher
20. "Vissi d'___", famous aria
21. Biblical verb
22. Supporter
23. Lacking authorization
24. Old World song thrush
26. In spite of the fact
27. ___ of Invisibility
28. Curtain plain-woven fabric
30. Shy or modest
31. Pro-Second Amendment grp.
33. Jared ___, actor
36. Japanese martial art.
37. Open-air Arabic market

39. Fell to one's knees
41. Share accumulating prog.
42. Fruity thirst quenchers
43. Just fine

44. Denotes unhealthy veggie
45. Harmless lie
47. Stock exch. debut
48. Bug
49. Life energy in Far East
50. Hit the ring floor

ANSWERS ON PAGE 239.

BEAUTY OF CHESS

ACROSS

1. Burial chamber
5. ___ Defense, chess opening
11. E.g., e.g
12. Great Plains native
13. Dentists' org.
14. Dandy
15. ___ sacrifice - over-the-board error: 2 wds.
18. Hardened
20. Rolled up
23. Pizza herb
27. Grocery chain
28. Conduit for a fluid
32. Global accounting body issuing professional certificates: abbr.
33. King's game US world champion: 2 wds
36. Gator relative
37. Lead
38. Drinking vessel
39. Forbidden by Islamic law
41. Nearsighted person
43. Failed state African country
47. Involving great risk: 2 wds.
50. ___ Damon, actor
54. ___ Dhabi, UAE capital

55. Wash'___ - hairstyling method: 2 wds.
56. Goes down
57. Qh8 or Re1 in Kasparov's book
58. Wall Street inits.

DOWN

1. Separated document page
2. British civil award: abbr.
3. Board member degree: abbr.
4. Robert de ___, king of Scotland
5. Goes into the pot
6. ___ pass : 2 wds.
7. State in the Rocky Mountains
8. Descartes' conclusion: 2 wds.
9. Sidewalk stand drink
10. Living cells vital coenzyme: abbr.
16. Hot ___
17. ___ Asimov, sci-fi author
19. Envelope line: abbr.
20. Peeling bark tree
21. Ancient Greek marketplace
22. Physical work
24. Noodlehead
25. Glaciate: 2 wds.

26. Garment size
29. Clock regulator: abbr.
30. Calgary Stampeders' org.
31. Teutonic war god
34. Immaterial money: 2 wds.
35. Right before final
40. Trim
42. Chinese official residence
44. Short skirt

45. Jason's craft
46. Seat ___, Spanish hatchback
47. ___ Solo, StarWars hero
48. Nigerian language
49. ___ feeling
51. Suffix with lull
52. Cookbook meas.
53. Double and get an insect

ANSWERS ON PAGE 239.

VERY COLD

ACROSS

1. Karate school
5. Extremely cold
12. Midterm or final
13. Imposed by authority
14. Reebok alternative
15. Bloodshed
16. A bid too high
18. Table linen
20. Old World Common Market: abbr.
23. Police radio call, for short
26. Intangible as air
31. Hop-drying kiln
33. One of the somatic sensations
35. Exotic holiday island
36. Vaporized
38. Off-road 4-wheeler, for short
40. Life-saving massage: abbr.
41. At all times
46. Exceptionally intelligent
50. Others, in Latin
53. Litter's smallest
54. Second most popular cryptocurr.
55. Drug buster
56. ___ zero - molecular activity stopper
57. Gaelic tongue

DOWN

1. Thermometer unit
2. Kitchenware brand
3. Place for candies
4. Premonition
5. Box office disaster
6. Four-star review
7. Still-life pitcher
8. ___ Efron, actor
9. Marsh elder
10. Soccer score (no goals)
11. Clumsy man
17. Swedish shug rug
19. Seniors' org.
21. ___ James, blues singer
22. Crab claw
24. Thick cushion
25. Relating to air pressure
27. Radiate
28. Brain scan: abbr.
29. Altar constellation
30. ___ Vegas
32. Ooze
34. Miniscule
35. ___ Streisand, singer
37. Solidified carbon dioxide: 2 wds.
39. Delivery vehicle
42. Stead or place
43. Light bulb unit
44. Flu symptom
45. Completely sensible

47. Unforeseen obstacle
48. Response: abbr.
49. "Am ___ blame?":
2 wds

51. White-handed gibbon
52. Tax collectors: abbr.

1	2	3	4		5	6	7		8	9	10	11
12					13				14			
15					16		17					
		18	19									
20	21	22						23	24	25		
26			27	28	29	30		31		32		
	33						34					
35				36								37
	38		39					40				
		41	42	43	44		45					
46	47	48	49					50	51	52		
53				54				55				
56								57				

101   ANSWERS ON PAGE 240.

MARVEL-OUS MOVIES

ACROSS

1. "___: The Dark World": 2013 film starring Chris Hemsworth

5. 3 on the phone

8. "The Incredible ___": 2008 film starring Lou Ferrigno

12. "Divorce capital," once

13. A hot time, in France

14. "___ penny, two a penny…"

15. Boats like the one Noah built

16. "... a lender be"

17. Architectural overhang

18. 2019 superhero film starring Brie Larson

21. Abbr. on a dashboard

22. Belgian painter James with "Scandalized Masks"

23. Arrange in advance

26. "Howards ___" (Forster novel)

27. "Fuzzy Wuzzy ___ a bear"

29. "Just the facts, ___"

30. Abbr. after a former military leader's name

31. Big name in building block toys

32. "Psychic" entertainer Geller

33. "All in favor" word

34. Coast Guard Academy student

35. Eyelash flutter

37. Bitterly cold

38. 2016 film starring Benedict Cumberbatch

43. Sean and Yoko

44. "___ a Most Unusual Day"

45. Epic poet

46. Baseball stitching

47. Brazil's ___ Paulo

48. "Idylls of the King" woman

49. Toward sunrise, in Mexico

50. "As needed," in Rx's

51. "And here you have it!"

DOWN

1. Gillette's ___ II razor

2. "Iliad" woman

3. Being punished, in a mess hall

4. Platform for public speaking

5. Blue jeans material

6. "Playing fields" place

7. State of unrest

8. Farmers tilling soil

9. Like promises never made

10. Power to influence people or things

11. "Kiss Kiss Bang Bang" critic Pauline

19. Angry Birds, for one

20. "___ the Band Played On" (1993 movie)

23. Campus in Dallas, TX

24. Hammer, anvil, and stirrup

25. Formal wear for Jeeves

26. AAA's opposite, in shoes

28. Falstaff, e.g.

30. Fiber-rich cracker brand

31. Wager

33. "It's ___-brainer!"

34. "Down on the Corner" band, affectionately

36. "Don't you recognize the voice?"

37. "I'm ready to rumble!"

38. Amount of medication

39. Red giant or white dwarf

40. "Peter Pan" pooch

41. You're filling one in

42. Norse epic

1	2	3	4		5	6	7		8	9	10	11
12					13				14			
15					16				17			
18				19				20				
			21				22					
23	24	25				26				27		28
29					30				31			
32				33				34				
	35		36				37					
38					39					40	41	42
43				44				45				
46				47				48				
49				50					51			

103

ANSWERS ON PAGE 240.

SWARM OF HONEYMAKERS

ACROSS

1. Ridicule in writting
8. Terminate
12. Corp. board member
13. Ireland, poetically
14. Unit of pressure
15. Web address
16. Expressed desire
17. West Coast oil company
18. Spore
20. High frilly woman headwear
22. Reporter's equipment, for short
23. The whole
24. Sampling plot used to study animal life
28. Lucifer
31. Part of the radiation spectrum: abbr.
32. Capture
34. Hawaiian side dish
35. Stationery brand
38. Lockjaw
41. Ozone-damaging gas: abbr.
43. Grayback
44. Small lump
47. Drink of the gods
51. Fume
52. Chinese nanny
54. Menagerie

55. ___ Pound, poet
56. Tender
57. ___ Ivanovic, tennis player
58. Observer
59. Make lovable

DOWN

1. Southern porgy
2. Bushy hairdo
3. Death ___ - casualties
4. Try anew
5. Triathlon competitor
6. Move at breakneck pace
7. Inside job
8. Maintaining equilibrium
9. Slightly truncated handheld **fire** source
10. Killer whale
11. Cement for a honeycomb structure
19. Smartwatch type of screen: abbr.
21. Outdated
24. Fertile egg-layer in a hive: 2 wds.
25. Insitution founded by Thos. Jefferson
26. Play the part
27. Make lacework

29. Remote access to corporate applications: abbr.
30. Promise to pay
33. ___ Shaw, Irish playwright
36. Part of an optical instrument
37. Patriots's org.
39. Giggle, titter: 2 wds.
40. Fox competitor
42. Bring to an end
45. Leaking out slowly
46. Grave
48. Pre-1917 ruler of Russia
49. Impressive: 2 wds.
50. Highway
53. Back-to-work day: abbr.

1	2	3		4	5	6	7		8	9	10	11
12				13					14			
15				16					17			
18			19				20	21				
		22				23						
24	25	26			27		28		29	30		
31				32		33			34			
35			36	37		38		39	40			
		41		42		43						
44	45	46				47			48	49	50	
51				52	53				54			
55				56					57			
58				59								

ANSWERS ON PAGE 240.

ARCHEOLOGY

ACROSS

1. Depositor's holding: abbr.
5. Italian peaks
9. British soccer player wife
12. Branch of Islam
13. Numbered on a plane
14. Euro precursor
15. Part of a gutter
16. Egyptian monuments
18. Evil spirits that prey upon sleepers
20. Christian ___, designer
21. Eisenhower's nickname
22. Rita ___, singer
24. Speed detector
27. Boss, in East Africa
29. Poker player mental state
30. Old Hellenic civilization: 2 wds.
34. Viscous stuff
35. Chinese mafia
36. Bangkok citizens
38. Big name in graphic cards manufacturing
39. Printer or monitor stat: abbr.
42. Essential for skiing
44. Make contact
46. Excavation site find
49. ___ breve (music term)

50. ___ culpa
51. Currency exchange fee
52. Stronghold
53. T-shirt size choices: abbr.
54. Bring up
55. Modify, revise

DOWN

1. Computer character coding set: abbr.
2. Solid piece
3. "Odyssey" sorceress
4. Forbidding prejudice: var.
5. Ambitious young person
6. Pasture
7. Buddy on the ranch
8. Single step
9. Unpleasantly eccentric person: var.
10. Sherlock's creator's monogram
11. ___ Hansen, Texas hold'em star
17. Protected by a deep trench
19. Riddick ___, boxer
23. Hollow in a bone
25. Intoxicating ingredient: abbr.
26. Road with a no.: abbr.

27. Nuclear weapons testing site
28. Political troublemaker
30. FBI employee, for short
31. Theater in Tokio or Osaka
32. By the sea
33. Barbarian attack
37. Up till now: 2 wds.
39. Parceled
40. Pointed Roman caps
41. Lacking skill
43. ___ war - start a conflict
45. In OK condition
46. Some radios
47. Deep sleep phase
48. US covert grp.

ANSWERS ON PAGE 240.

PAINTINGS

ACROSS

1. Put down
4. Successful move
8. Scottish legendary pirate, Captain William ___
12. ''I knew it!''
13. Very hard to find
14. UN civil aviation agency using four-letter codes: abbr.
15. Work of art dealing with evening or night
17. Microwave
18. Defensive earthwork
19. Inc., in London
21. Canyon sound
25. To urge or call by shouting
29. When repeated, a dance
32. Your and my
33. Run ___ of the law
34. Summer month
35. Allowed by law
37. Blue
38. Beg
40. "Aladdin" prince
41. Bottom line
42. Painting holder
43. Tidy
45. Coloring substance
47. Charitable donations

50. Dry riverbed
53. Mona Lisa, e.g.
57. October birthstone
58. Compressed data, briefly
59. Employ
60. Sea eagle
61. Egyptian Christian
62. Cannes award, Palme ___

DOWN

1. Picture of countryside
2. Greeting at sea
3. Talk on and on: var.
4. Wine classification, Grand ___
5. Paddle
6. Coffee vessel
7. Spa treatment
8. More or less: 2 wds.
9. Critical hosp. area
10. Divided US territory
11. Buck's mate
16. Golf peg
20. Greek Muse of comedy
22. Without emotion
23. Shade of color
24. Heart or stomach, e.g.
26. Tax write-off
27. Hawaiian feast
28. Great painter: 2 wds.
30. Storytelling dance
31. Forever and a day

36. Ginger ___
39. Old Roman magistrate
44. Driveway surface
46. Monumental
48. Glorify
49. Japanese soup
50. Misery

51. Earth Day mo.
52. Karate grade
54. Lennon's love
55. Declaration of purchasing intent: abbr.
56. Little kid

ANSWERS ON PAGE 241.

WINTER FLYING SPORT

ACROSS

1. U.F.C. fighting style
4. Highest point
8. Alone
12. Alternative to the pill: abbr.
13. Thin cut
14. Organic compound
15. Norm: abbr.
16. Rear end
17. Red shade
18. Ski jump referee points: 2 wds.
21. Craft
22. ___ Francisco
23. More than buzzed
26. Nuclear physicics Nobelist, Enrico ___
29. Method for increasing the web traffic: abbr.
30. Informer
32. Five-rings logo org.
33. Limestone formation
36. Nigerian language
39. Hasten
41. Photog's item: abbr.
42. Arrival zone for Matti Nykanen, e.g.: 2 wds.
47. No longer mint
49. Flair
50. ER notation
51. Wizard, old-style
52. Large prefix

53. 12, to 4 and 6: math abbr.
54. Trudge
55. Figure-skating jump
56. Age-determining stat

DOWN

1. Fail to see
2. Mixed breed
3. GPS input, slangily
4. To the rear
5. Grouping
6. Catchall category: abbr.
7. Cultural spirit
8. Peaceful
9. Burden
10. High tennis shot
11. ___ Games
19. Chinese philosopher, ___-tzu
20. UK fliers: abbr.
23. Mermaid's home
24. Rocky pinnacle
25. Dawn to dusk
27. Chest bone
28. Extinct bird of New Zealand
29. One of the winter sports: 2 wds.
31. Cargo capacity
34. Out of the sun
35. Pewter component
37. Monarch-related
38. "That's awful!"

40. Swelling
42. Toy block brand
43. Holm oak
44. Without purpose

45. Bonkers
46. Young sheep
48. Baseball's Bando

ANSWERS ON PAGE 241.

GRETA GERWIG

ACROSS

1. Got off the ground
5. "A Series of Unfortunate Events" villain Count __
9. "Chocolate" dog, for short
12. 1969 Creedence Clearwater Revival hit
13. Grow wearisome
14. Hoppy-hour order?
15. Basically alike
16. Faulkner femme fatale __ Varner
17. Bit of Seurat painting
18. Greta Gerwig is a veterinary nurse in this 2016 dark comedy with Danny DeVito and Julie Delpy
20. "But of course!"
21. "CSI" sample
22. Development site
24. Bug on a plant
27. Authentic
30. Billet-__ (love letter)
31. Bounder
32. "Jurassic Park" character
33. Part mortal and part deity
35. Drops off the grid, say
36. Beehive-raiding beast
37. Any relative
38. Night flyer
40. Gerwig stars in and co-wrote this 2012 comedy directed by companion Noah Baumbach
45. Dish of roasted roots
46. Pate de __ gras
47. "And others," in lists
48. Flying fish-eater
49. Icelandic literary work
50. Bring down, as a house
51. It gives one good standing?
52. A saxophone has one
53. Bump on a lid

DOWN

1. Diamond defect
2. Mischief-maker of Norse myth
3. "Nurse Jackie" star Falco
4. Southern grocery chain
5. "Einstein on the Beach," for one
6. Give kudos to
7. Gave permission
8. Large wine bottle
9. This 2017 coming-of-age film was nominated for five Oscars

10. Additive to some soaps
11. Many are placed in Vegas
19. Bring to a conclusion
23. Rebels against Queeg
24. "Just __ water"
25. "The Bells" writer
26. Gerwig co-stars with Al Pacino in this 2014 comedy-drama (with "The")
27. __ about (roam)
28. "Her maiden name was" word

29. George Strait's "All My __ Live in Texas"
31. Eat away at
34. Lighting electrician on a set
35. Involuntary sound
37. Do a bread-making chore
38. Autobahn vehicle
39. Put on, as a uniform
41. Adjutant, e.g.
42. "ER" exclamation
43. Foggy
44. Away from the breeze

ANSWERS ON PAGE 241.

STAY HEALTHY

ACROSS

1. Wind dir.
4. Grease
8. Carpenter's groove
12. Nourishment
14. Govt. voting agcy.
15. Took the lid off
16. Winter glider
17. Trendy
18. Put in jail: 2 wds
21. TV's "Science Guy", Bill
   ___
23. Rwandan tribe
25. Stratagem
27. "Larger ___ life"
30. Pampering, briefly
31. Apple product
32. Black gold
33. Hunt for
34. Not sweet (wine)
35. The "A" in A.D.
36. Low card
37. Make curly
39. Thurman of ''Pulp Fiction"
41. False front
44. Flight coordinators: abbr.
47. E___ virus
48. Prophetic
51. Campaigner, for short
52. Healthy
53. Pastoral poem: var.

54. Study of the stars: abbr.
55. "Nova" network

DOWN

1. Cold-shoulder
2. Nearest star
3. Engrave
4. Impudent
5. Roger Federer's org.
6. Cambodian money
7. Wonderland bird
9. Excited
10. REM stage: 2 wds.
11. Med. condition with repetitive behavior: abbr.
13. Showered
16. Merchandise ID: abbr.
19. UPS unit: abbr.
20. Goji berries or kale
22. Prince William's school
24. Gross
25. Computer architecture acronym: abbr.
26. ___ accepted norm
28. VIN for vessels
29. Baseball family name
33. Social standing
35. Therapists' org.
38. Longtime Elton John label
40. Pepper gun sprayer
42. Capital of Qatar

114

43. God of love
45. Hoof sound
46. Greek god of war
47. Electronic storage

density measure: abbr.
49. PC key
50. Embassy VIP: abbr.

1	2	3		4	5	6	7		8	9	10	11
12			13							14		
15									16			
		17					18		19				
	20		21		22			23				24
25		26				27	28	29			30	
31						32				33		
34				35						36		
37			38					39	40			
	41				42	43		44		45		46
47					48		49				50	
51				52								
53					54					55		

TERMINATOR-LIKE FUTURE

ACROSS

1. Italian sparkling wine, ___ Spumante
5. UN nuclear watchdog agcy.
9. Monk's title
12. Economical
13. ''Fine by me"
14. Paris street
15. Knowledge of one's own individuality: 2 wds.
18. New York lake
19. Facts and figures
20. Decent: 2 wds.
24. Confronted
28. ___ de Janeiro
29. Shark part
32. Line between countries
34. Former Portugese coin
36. Expert
37. Dashboard abbr.
39. Wise Athenian lawgiver
40. Inability to recall the names of objects
43. Enthusiastic about
45. Medium-hot curry
50. Brain-like cluster of computer processors: 2 wds.
54. Family vehicle
55. Cutting remark
56. Sheltered, nautically
57. "The best things in life ___ free"
58. Kournikova of tennis
59. Cut the crop

DOWN

1. As well
2. Caught in the act
3. Story
4. Fastened firmly
5. Hawkeye
6. Alias preceder
7. Musical talent
8. Affirmative vote
9. Terrible
10. Expel
11. Tableland
16. Billboard
17. Confidentiality document: abbr.
21. Alternatively
22. Father's Day gift
23. Manager
24. Lawyers and judges org.
25. Youngest woman to serve in Congress, familiarly
26. Beast
27. Sample
30. Phrase of commitment: 2 wds.
31. Opposite of "oui"
33. Engine speed: abbr.

35. US-USSR tension: 2 wds.
38. Conversation starter
41. Neither's partner
42. Amorphous creature
43. Machu Picchu builder
44. Within reach
46. Email address symbol
47. Part to play

48. Region
49. Round straw basket
51. Fabric woven from camel hair
52. System of connected PCs
53. "You don't have to write me back", shortly

ANSWERS ON PAGE 242.

THAT'S A NO-NO

ACROSS

1. Sailors
5. Frequently, in verse
8. Medal recipient
12. Away from shore
13. Kiboshed
15. Influence unfairly
16. Santana's first hit, 1970
17. "In all probability..."
19. Alternative to nothing
20. 20-vol. lexicon
21. Actor ___ Elba of "The Wire"
23. Start of Mr. Rogers' song
26. Creator of lofty lines
27. Foster, as wrongdoing
28. Disallowed
31. Not permitted
33. "Peter and the Wolf" duck
34. Chemically inactive
36. Abdomen, in slang
37. Instructional sequence
38. Couple in Cancun
41. 1958-1961 alliance
43. Fairies and pixies, e.g.
45. Napoleonic leader?
48. "Nasty" first name in tennis
49. Not legal
50. "Hello, Dolly!" lead role
51. Part of Ali's record
52. Fleur de ___
53. First place?

DOWN

1. Prohibited
2. Line to the audience
3. Check the total of
4. Attitude
5. Went too far
6. High temperatures
7. Angle or cycle starter
8. Allen Ginsberg beat poem
9. And elsewhere: Lat.
10. "Star Wars: The Force Awakens" girl
11. Carry-___ (airplane totes)
14. "Gil ___" (Le Sage novel)
18. Assistant on the Hill
22. "Definitely maybe"
24. A golfer puts it in the ground
25. Benchmark, briefly
26. Bill below five
27. "Guest" at certain meals
28. Cranberry "field"
29. "Aladdin" monkey
30. Unfit for
32. British Isles tongue

35. Anthony who sang "What Kind of Fool **Am** I"
37. Mlle. from Acapulco
38. Distributed bit by bit
39. "Drab" army color

40. Ball of yarn
42. Feels a bit punk
44. Dossier
45. Army sleeper
46. Arctic diver
47. Belt hole maker

ANSWERS ON PAGE 242.

NAVAL WARFARE

ACROSS

1. Type of warship
7. Sorcery
11. No longer fresh
12. Maori word for a ritualised revenge to restore balance
13. Of service
15. Ringo of the Beatles
17. 12th Jewish month
18. Less dusty
20. Serving to symbolize
22. "If only ___ listened..."
23. Prefix for the birds
24. Kind of drive: 2 wds.
26. Hint
27. Michelangelo work
30. Destroyer
33. Bulg. neighbor
34. Tropical disease
36. WWII battle site, ___ Jima
37. Brain cover, ___ mater
38. Prefix with "structure" or "red"
42. Obtaining
44. Came down to earth: var.
45. Spring up
46. Simple egg-shaped wind instrument
49. Winery vessel
50. Calf, to a cowboy

51. Manicurist's board
52. Commander in chief of a navy

DOWN

1. Container for oil or vinegar
2. Exhaust: 2 wds.
3. Sloping letters
4. Day of rest: abbr.
5. Building add-on
6. Repeat again, like a sound
7. Pondered
8. Lead-in to "girl!" or "boy!"
9. Llama relative
10. Transporter of disease
14. Devious
16. Musical show
19. Madagascar tree climber
21. Epidemic-fighting agcy.
25. Violin bow coating
27. Type of warship
28. Boat mover
29. Eliciting feeling
31. Easter Island: Rapa ___
32. Ancient Roman coins
35. Chinese temple
37. Devotion
39. Pilot
40. ___ Tin Tin
41. In any way: 2 wds.

43. Russian emperor
47. Atlantic food fish

48. Corporate yearly gathering: abbr.

IN THE OPERA

ACROSS

1. Pre-Euro Spanish currency
6. Hound's trail
11. Military no-show: abbr.
12. Shutter part
13. Site of London's Royal Opera House: 2 wds.
16. Last letter of the Hebrew alphabet, similar to the letter T
17. Online break-in
18. Gun the motor, for short
20. Breed of terrier
22. Canada's ___ Island National Park
23. Blow away
24. Omega-3 fatty acid: abbr.
26. Inventor and manufacturer of the sewing machine, Isaac ___
29. Compound derived from ammonia
32. Shabby
33. Last piece of music
35. D.C. United org
36. "Awesome!"
37. Inflation indicator: abbr.
39. Gentle
43. 180 degrees from NNE

44. Throat-clearing sound
45. Reagan's "Star Wars" prog.
46. Relating to large cities
50. Gourmet's sense
51. One-person performances
52. Bridges of Hollywood
53. Obliquely: var.

DOWN

1. Ancient Britons
2. Shrewd
3. Lamb's mother
4. Heavy weight
5. 50s tennis legend: ___ Gibson
6. Casual pants
7. Pig meat
8. Arab lute
9. Surplus amount
10. Extended, as a membership
14. Sturdy tree
15. Guy's counterpart
19. Extremely
21. Icelandic poetry
25. Norse underworld queen
27. Manhattan, e.g.: abbr.
28. "Untouchable" Eliot
29. Accounting standards issued by IASB: abbr.
30. Corruptive atmosphere

31. Live inside, as a spirit
34. Resounded
35. Brunch cocktail
38. Energy
40. Port city of ancient Rome

41. Rx overseer
42. Add a bit of color
44. Pretentious
47. Chinese principle
48. The "L" of L.A.
49. Sort

ANSWERS ON PAGE 242.

VOLCANIC ACTIVITY

ACROSS

1. Prefix with cycle
4. Three wise men
8. Craving
12. Japanese computer giant
13. Sacred image: var.
14. Corn Belt state
15. "___ Got a Secret"
16. ''That's mine!"
17. Abbr. at the end of a list: 2 wds.
18. Shifting part of the earth's crust: 2 wds.
21. Harry Potter's best friend
22. Disencumber
23. Not shallow
25. Englishman, for short
26. Race unit
29. US state with the highest number of lava emitters
31. Dark volcanic rock
33. "Let me think..."
34. Just lying around
35. Cocoon inhabitant
36. Beatty of "Deliverance"
37. Helping hand
38. Mt. Wrangell, e.g.: 2 wds.
45. Frighten away birds
46. Fearless

47. Instruction books, How-___
48. Poetic foot
49. Mah-jongg piece
50. Fireworks reaction
51. At liberty
52. Practice in the ring
53. Genetic info carrier: abbr.

DOWN

1. One
2. "Scream" star, ___ Campbell
3. Frozen dessert: 2 wds.
4. Cricketing position: 2 wds.
5. Blood-related
6. Mongolian desert
7. Engrave or write upon
8. Brandish
9. Letter after theta
10. Police jacket letters
11. In good health
19. First-rate
20. Hummus holder
23. Morse code sound
24. Nightmarish street
25. They're unlikely to be collected: 2 wds.
26. Someone who praises highly
27. Swiss peak
28. School org.

30. Ukraine's capital city
32. Household cleanser, ___ & Span
36. Weeper of Greek myth
37. Tree with catkins
38. "In your dreams!": 2 wds.

39. Burn slightly
40. Heavy reading
41. Internet phone calling
42. Earthenware pot
43. Lunch time
44. Dept. of Labor agency

ANSWERS ON PAGE 243.

SAOIRSE RONAN MOVIES

ACROSS

1. Fanciful notion
5. "Little Orphan Annie" character (with "The")
8. Bulletin board fastener
12. "King of the road" vagabond
13. British track star Sebastian
14. Bouffant, for one
15. Astra or Vectra maker
16. What the Mohs scale measures
18. Ronan plays Rat in this 2019 dark fairy tale
20. Dutch engineering feat
21. "The ___ Couple"
22. Onetime honor for cable TV shows
25. Common Hawaiian dish
28. 2017 fully painted animated feature with Saoirse Ronan as van Gogh's friend Marguerite
31. 180 degrees from WSW
32. Ushered
33. Beginning of a laugh
35. Bonheur or Parks
36. Ronan's character is a bloodsucker on the run in this 2012 feature

39. Upper-class wealth
41. Appetizer in Barcelona
44. Animal shelter
45. "Mind the ___" (Underground warning)
46. Administered with a spoon, perhaps
47. 1980s PCs
48. Bard's "before"
49. Abbr. on a food container

DOWN

1. "Horton Hears a ___" (Dr. Seuss story)
2. "___ on Pop" (Dr. Seuss book)
3. Revival tent cry
4. Island home of Father Damien
5. Berliner's eight
6. Emulate an eagle
7. Kind of table in chemistry class
8. Adjusted guitar strings
9. Copycat
10. Audiophile collection
11. Beats in the ring, for short
17. Netflix delivery
19. Already stitched
20. Brand of bug killer
22. "Game of Thrones" beverage

23. Info on a toy package
24. Campers, briefly
25. Chain with day care
26. ___-day (kind of multivitamin)
27. "___ be a pleasure!" ("Love to!")
29. Seaweed for sushi rolls
30. Caesar salad ingredient
33. Church songs
34. Nitrogen: Prefix
36. Place to sleep in an apt.
37. A stone's throw away
38. A or O, at the blood bank
39. "Mikado" sash
40. Chemist's hangout
42. A hand for Snoopy
43. Key on either side of the space bar

ANSWERS ON PAGE 243.

GETTING MARRIED

ACROSS

1. Church section
5. Wolf's sound
9. On agenda, yet not warranted: abbr.
12. Seed coat
13. Grand
14. Italy's equivalent of the BBC: ___ Uno
15. Wedding follower
17. Baseball great Mel
18. Hair goo
19. Not chronic
21. Country west of Egypt
24. Army division
26. Hockey legend: Bobby ___
27. Jockey's strap
29. Fungal spore cases
32. Ornamental carp
33. Bottom point
35. Poetic dusk
36. ___- European languages
38. ___ good example: 2 wds.
39. Pop-ups, e.g.
40. Great Swiss mathematician, "Elements of Algebra" author
42. Spread the news
44. Montana city

46. TV schedule abbr.
47. Back then
48. Date of the wedding: 3 wds.
54. Priest's robe
55. "Poker Face" singer, Lady ___
56. Gaelic name for Ireland
57. Caustic substance
58. What the nose knows
59. It's outstanding

DOWN

1. Sound of relief
2. Experienced
3. Transgression
4. Mournful poem
5. WWW code
6. "So that's your game!"
7. Romance
8. Moon-related
9. The clothes, linen and jewelry of a bride
10. Sheet of matted cotton or wool
11. Quote
16. Long for
20. Tax pro: abbr.
21. Norse trickster god
22. Clothes presser
23. Give her a ring: 3 wds.
24. Autumn drink
25. "I'm working ___ !": 2 wds.

128

28. Alleviate
30. Ghana money
31. Research facil.
34. Synagogue leader
37. Not at home
41. Discharge: 2 wds.
43. Stormed
44. False god

45. Hideous
46. Skier's transport
49. Used to own
50. Self-image
51. Expire
52. Wall St. Figure: abbr.
53. "Are we there ___ ?"

1	2	3	4		5	6	7	8		9	10	11
12					13					14		
15				16						17		
			18					19	20			
21	22	23				24	25					
26				27	28				29		30	31
32				33			34		35			
36			37		38				39			
		40		41				42	43			
44	45					46						
47				48	49	50				51	52	53
54				55					56			
57				58					59			

ANSWERS ON PAGE 243.

ECOLOGY

ACROSS

1. Not "dis"
4. Piece of merchandise
8. Computer graphics format: abbr.
11. Snug and comfy
12. Hertz Rent -___-___
13. Goddess who rescued Odysseus
14. Composer's creation
15. Start of a summer shower
17. Eco-friendly kind of engine: 2 wds.
19. Crooner, ___ King Cole
20. And so on: abbr.
22. Game of Thrones' airer
25. "Evita" narrator
27. Popular frozen-dessert chain
30. Our "mother"
32. H2O
33. Cloth-eating insect
34. Matador's shout
36. "I told you so!"
37. Sound at the door
40. ___ de Cologne
42. Variety of plant and animal life
48. Flounce, frill
49. Magician's opening
50. 401(k) alternative
51. "Star Wars" princess
52. Nerd
53. MD for women: abbr.
54. Small whirlpool
55. File extension that runs programs

DOWN

1. Inside info
2. French Riviera: Cote d'___
3. "Iron Mike"
4. Hospitality
5. ''Super-food" berry
6. Lift
7. Young's partner in accounting
8. Annual cycling race: ___ d'Italia
9. Privy to: 2 wds.
10. Dandy
11. Unc's kid
16. Formal rulings
18. A pop
21. Instrument for Orpheus
22. Cannabis plant
23. Chinese steamed bun
24. Leftover
26. "The Name of the Rose" author, Umberto ___
28. Dol. fractions
29. Honey maker
31. Pulsate
32. Have on

35. Margin for error
38. "Someone Like You" singer
39. Heaped
41. Practical application
42. Inter

43. Persia, today
44. Empty space
45. Mountain goat
46. Genealogy diagram
47. Chatter
48. Least bit: abbr.

DENTAL HEALTH

ACROSS

1. Prompter
6. Perfect rating
9. Part of H.R.H.
12. "Rigoletto" composer, Giuseppe ___
13. One of the four bases of DNA
15. Small and round, like birds' eyes
16. Medical examination
17. Biblical ark builder
19. Verb with "thou"
20. Bermuda hrs.
22. "Blowin' in the Wind" singer, Bob ___
25. "V for Vendetta" actor, Stephen ___
26. Molar cleaner
29. Spelling of "Beverly Hills 90210"
30. Mins. and mins.
31. Ocean Spray flavor prefix
35. Avoidance
38. Not in the office in 2020: abbr.
41. Related on the mother's side
42. N.Y. Mets' div
43. African antelope
45. Deer sir
47. Coffee request: 2 wds.

50. City in Oklahoma
53. Bruise, injure
54. Distrustful
55. Treats symptoms associated with menopause: abbr.
56. Yoga surface
57. John of England

DOWN

1. Sunscreen letters
2. "Riddle-me-___"
3. Researcher's benefactor
4. Taro root
5. Capital of Saudi Arabia
6. Middle X or O
7. "Th" in Old English
8. "You ___bother!"
9. Trail user
10. Busy: 2 wds.
11. Nasal dividers
14. Sgt., e.g.
18. Dash-like punctuation mark
20. Lawyer: abbr.
21. Great Lakes canal
23. First stage of an insect
24. Valuable items
27. Hint
28. Prefix for "outside"
32. Curl of hair
33. "You've got mail" co.
34. Opposite SSW

36. Australian eucalyptus: 2 wds.

37. Stinging plant

38. Serving girl

39. Elevator stop

40. Lacks

44. Pistachio, e.g.

46. "The Clan of the Cave Bear" author

48. Simile words: 2 wds

49. No longer working: abbr.

51. No seats' sign

52. "The Fountainhead" author, ___ Rand

ANSWERS ON PAGE 244.

___ HO!

ACROSS

1. "Field of Dreams" setting
5. Getting on
8. Whip
12. Sporty car roof
13. Seven, on a sundial
14. Diva's solo
15. Farmer's acreage
17. Break a habit
18. Buddy of rock fame
19. Harry Potter's country
21. "___ and whose army?"
23. Baby's "piggy"
24. "Que Sera, Sera" singer Doris
27. Apprehend, as a perp
29. Basket twig
33. A round cheese
35. Free (of)
37. A few or more
38. Dried coconut meat
40. Auction gesture
42. Bar bowl item
43. Audiophile's collection
45. Acrobat catcher
47. Floral crown
51. Norman Bates is a good example of one
55. A lake or canal
56. New Zealand's most populous city
58. "At Last" singer James
59. Navy noncom
60. "Good heavens!"
61. "Peachy ___!"
62. Barrel at a bash
63. Boomers' kids, briefly

DOWN

1. Calamine lotion target
2. Another, in Madrid
3. Blanket material
4. Put on, as makeup
5. Caesar's eggs
6. "I Walk the ___," Cash hit
7. Failed to do
8. Like the Wild West of yore
9. Conspiracy buff's ___ 51
10. Actress Phillips of "I, Claudius"
11. Clock part
16. Home to French silk makers
20. Baby talk word
22. '50s Mideast alliance
24. Big mo. for toy stores
25. "Much ___ About Nothing"
26. Bark annoyingly
28. Bargain holder, maybe
30. Atom with a charge
31. Aussie coat-of-arms bird

32. Like professors emeritus: abbr.
34. Magic Eraser spokesman
36. "American Pie" McLean
39. "Give Kids A Smile" org.
41. Newspaper's city ___
44. Cheese and crackers, e.g.
46. Bathroom-cleaner brand
47. Adorkable one
48. Commedia dell'___ (improvised comedy)
49. Baptism or confirmation, e.g.
50. Copy, for short
52. Actor Nicolas
53. Burl in wood
54. "Against All ___" (Phil Collins #1 hit)
57. Gear piece

 ANSWERS ON PAGE 244.

IN THE VINEYARD

ACROSS

1. Stick in one's ___
5. Adverse criticism
9. Taoism founder, Lao- ___
12. "Take one!"
13. Straight row
14. Snakelike fish
15. Water, in Mexico
16. Chardonnay adjective
17. "The Matrix" role
18. Not intended for wine production: 2 wds.
21. Fill with joy
22. Dined at home
24. Coat-of-arms expert
28. Scannable product ID: abbr.
31. Invoice fig.
32. Shooting marble
34. You might say: 3 wds.
39. Pompous walk
40. Largest moon of Saturn
43. The growing of grapes
47. Asian country, ___ Lanka
49. USA part
50. Amorphous shape
51. Elementary particle
52. Diminish
53. Old school or college, ___ mater
54. Reply envelope: abbr.

55. Architectural pier
56. Reverse, e.g.

DOWN

1. French castle
2. Kingly, royal
3. Curacao neighbor
4. Fortune
5. Thrash
6. Dishonest person
7. Singer: Paul ___
8. Telephone panel
9. Stretched to the limit
10. Last of 26
11. Rating system in competitive chess
19. Wide shoe spec
20. Life in outer space: abbr.
23. "Give ___ go": 2 wds.
25. Dorm VIPs
26. Current unit: abbr.
27. 4G ___: mobile device standard
29. L.A. clock setting
30. Like a crow
33. Venue for a tasting: 2 wds.
35. Honey-eating bird of NZ
36. Canadian capital
37. US/Eur divider: abbr.
38. Knapsack: 2 wds.
41. Gown fabric

42. Fragrance
44. Single-named supermodel
45. Small change
46. Common fertilizer compound
47. Bro's sibling
48. Profitability ratio on balance sheet: abbr.

ANSWERS ON PAGE 244.

ITALIAN FOOD

ACROSS

1. Dance party enthusiast
6. Afternoon hrs.
9. Tour org.
12. Express a viewpoint
13. Island guitar, for short
14. Sea eagle
15. Long pasta
17. Spanish hero: El ___
18. No less than: 2 wds.
19. Polish money
21. Barbell abbr.
22. Coffin frame
23. Police
26. City on the Yangtze: var.
29. Other form of Roger that in military slang: abbr.
30. "Nothing ___ !"
32. "Platoon" setting, briefly
33. Like a young lady
35. Bean used to make miso
36. Bulk
37. Agitated (with "up")
39. Performs, old-style
41. Quite a few
45. "How cute!" sounds
46. Pizza sausage
48. Anti-narcotics org.
49. Simon & Garfunkel "I ___ Rock": 2 wds.
50. Military survey
51. Common girl's middle name
52. Convent dweller
53. Linked, as oxen

DOWN

1. Santa ___ , California
2. Scheduled mtg.
3. Lab vessel
4. Karl Marx collaborator
5. Post-op time
6. Golf stroke
7. NYSE or NASDAQ: abbr.
8. Confiscating
9. Italian sheep's cheese
10. Sand
11. Pop artist, ___Warhol
16. Serpentine letter
20. Albanian money
22. Embargo
23. Abbr. on a receipt
24. French word for "yes"
25. Hard Italian cheese
26. US biomedical research agcy.
27. Aye's opposite
28. ABC a.m. show
30. Type of hands
31. C.I.A. predecessor
34. Back muscle, for short

35. Not mono
37. Cool, like a cat
38. Each one
39. Baby's first word
40. Gil in "Midnight in Paris", ___ Wilson
41. Reach across
42. Large stone
43. Suffix with appear
44. Wasn't honest
47. Australian runners

1	2	3	4	5		6	7	8		9	10	11
12						13				14		
15					16					17		
18							19	20				
			21				22					
23	24	25				26					27	28
29				30	31					32		
33			34					35				
		36					37	38				
39	40					41				42	43	44
45				46	47				50			
48				49					50			
51				52					53			

ANSWERS ON PAGE 244.

HIGH IN THE MOUNTAINS

ACROSS

1. Some small batteries
5. Lettuce
8. Hospital division
12. After-bath powder
13. Facing: abbr.
14. One of the Great Lakes
15. Deadly shark
16. Light equipment for miner and speleologist: 2 wds.
18. Car
20. Key
21. 1945 conference site
23. Obi, e.g.
25. Software intermediary that allows two applications to talk to each other: abbr.
26. European flatfish
28. "Ghost" psychic ___ Mae Brown
31. Hiking boot with a lug sole
32. Snoop
33. English assignment
34. British recording giant
35. Lawyer: abbr.
36. "Tomorrow" singer
38. Sound
41. Pub offerings
42. Spikes on boots for climbing

45. Mountain pass in India
48. Fourth dimension
49. "I don't think so"
50. Wander
51. Lenovo or Dell competitor
52. Kids-show rating
53. Newspaper page

DOWN

1. Money dispenser
2. High bond rating
3. To make less acidic
4. Talent finder
5. Pacific salmon
6. Reveal, in poetry
7. Place to relax
8. From Cardiff
9. Asia's shrinking Sea
10. Icy coating
11. Co. division
17. Unfaithful
19. Place for card games
21. Harsh cry
22. On ___ with, equal to: 2 wds.
23. Oscar winner, Mary ___ Spacek
24. Utah ski resort
27. Relax
28. Workplace with non-union members: 2 wds.
29. "GI Jane" star, ___ Moore

30. Grammy winner, India
___

35. Archer, at times
37. Opposite of blanco
38. Official records
39. Acid type that can cause gout

40. Title for Judi Dench
41. Grayish
43. Hudson Bay prov.
44. Part of USNA: abbr.
46. "___ Maria"
47. "Ideas worth spreading" org.

ANSWERS ON PAGE 245.

MEDIEVAL CAVALRY CLASH

ACROSS

1. Baseball stat.
4. Mexican peninsula
8. Criminal
12. Chain email: abbr.
13. Got 100% on
14. Arizona Indian
15. Incapacitated
17. Designer, ___ Saint Laurent
18. Medieval knight contest
20. Greeting in "Winnie the Pooh"
23. North Pole explorer, Richard ___
24. Largest continent
25. Commoner
29. Unhorse, heavy cavalry, lance, where
34. Safecracker
35. On-line read, briefly
36. Summit
39. Cheap cigar: var.
40. Protection for a knight
44. Palm starch
45. Madhouse, informally
49. Plant stalk
50. Russian pancake
51. OPEC unit: abbr.
52. Conservative Brit.
53. Partner in war
54. Mercedes competitor

DOWN

1. "Mayberry ___"
2. D.C. area airport: abbr.
3. Fingerprints
4. Hindu gentleman: var.
5. Legal rights org.
6. Mock
7. Annex: abbr.
8. Smell of a lamb dish
9. Hang in the air
10. Overturn
11. Main point
16. Book of maps
19. "Dancing Queen" group
20. Pilgrimage to Mecca
21. Japan's largest active volcano
22. "Kill Bil" actress, Lucy ___
25. Cobbler's cousin
26. Kind of compressed fuel: abbr.
27. Bird-to-be
28. Shrewd
30. Kid
31. Take another shot
32. Punk rock subgenre
33. Pester
36. Teacher of Aristotle
37. Avid
38. Mote

39. One of the Corleone boys
40. "Check this out!"
41. "Sin City" actress, Jessica ___
42. Bakery product
43. Drudgery
46. Consumer protection org.
47. Big Blue
48. Dodgers' division

ANSWERS ON PAGE 245.

BARREN AND LIFELESS

ACROSS

1. Elton John, e.g.
4. Run out of a container
9. Dadaism founder, Jean ___
12. Prefix with center
13. Bustles
14. Ripken of baseball
15. Barren area
17. ___ Longoria of "Desperate Housewives"
18. Buckeye State
19. Guitar part
20. Boca ___ , Florida
22. Elevate in rank
24. Morse code sound
25. Fishing basket
26. Deserted and neglected
31. Buenos ___ , Argentina
32. More, in Mexico
34. Make believe
37. River near Nottingham, UK
39. Auld lang syne
40. Testify
41. Losing line in tic-tac-toe
42. Lifeless marsh: 2 wds.
45. T.G.I.F. part
46. Aquarium problem
47. "Skip to My ___"
48. Hurricane's center
49. Genesis
50. Immerse

DOWN

1. Alaska's purchaser
2. Hoppy beer, briefly
3. Italian dish cooked in broth
4. Oktoberfest souvenir
5. Horseback game
6. Actress, Lupino of "High Sierra"
7. Isolation
8. Hallucinogen: abbr.
9. Sharp
10. Bolero composer
11. Shallow dish
16. However, briefly
19. People
21. Insurance company
22. Made a mistake
23. Museum funding org.
25. Midwestern farmland: 2 wds.
27. Romantic meeting
28. "A pox on you!"
29. Shade of green
30. Indian flatbread
33. Increase: 2 wds.
34. Creeping evergreen shrub
35. Like soil around big trees

144

36. Not smooth
37. Tube: 2 wds.
38. VCR button
40. Sixth Jewish month

42. German article, "Der, die, ___"
43. Old-fashioned stove, most popular in UK
44. Miss Piggy's word

ANSWERS ON PAGE 245.

MISHMASH

ACROSS

1. Minor battle
5. Army food
9. Cattle thief
10. Boot out, as a tenant
11. Pointer (often ignored)
12. Get together
13. Potential wild cards
16. Group behind many a roast
19. "Star Wars" good guys
20. Embarrassment
21. Biting remark
22. They make miniatures

DOWN

1. Flapjack topper
2. Look over carefully
3. Fireman's badge shape
4. Place to pick up a kitten
6. Creole-speaking nation
7. 1985 film set in Amish country
8. World leaders
12. Found work
14. Blow up, as a picture
15. Pampas cowboy
17. Influential tribe member
18. Christmas bonanza

ANSWERS ON PAGE 245.

PC HARDWARE

ACROSS

1. "___ , humbug!"
4. Not up yet
8. Radar signal
12. It's next to nothing
13. Elvis film, "___ Las Vegas"
14. Adult nits
15. Took the cookie, say
16. Pizzeria fixture
17. Consumer
18. Primary component of all computing devices: 2 wds.
21. Romanian coin
22. Ages and ages, in geology
23. Medicative shampoo ingredient: 2 wds.
27. Encourage: 2 wds.
30. Weird, magical
31. Upper limit
33. Pitcher's stat
34. Cat calls
37. Well-mannered
40. Fortune or chance, old style
42. Drag with a car
43. Main computer component
48. Shade of blue
50. TV's "American ___"

51. Chesapeake or San Francisco, e.g.
52. Demonic
53. Malaria symptom
54. Tell a whopper
55. Be dependent
56. Not as much
57. "Star Trek" rank: abbr.

DOWN

1. Squeezers
2. Strongly against
3. Part of a shoe
4. Long-legged shore bird
5. Temporary camp for soldiers
6. Not bumpy
7. Move to music
8. Old bleach alternative
9. Speech problem
10. "Rocks"
11. Private
19. Feeling poorly
20. Garden tool
23. Alan Turing's child
24. Praiseful poem
25. Big deal
26. Dust remover
28. "Gosh!"
29. Mining extract
32. Like rock or stone
35. Entirely
36. Warmed the bench
38. Titled ones

39. Duo
41. Small medicine bottle
43. Sent or received
44. Brim, border
45. Skillful

46. Reason for postponement
47. Colorants
49. First woman

ANSWERS ON PAGE 246.

MATT DAMON MOVIES

ACROSS

1. "Hey there, matey!"
5. "Nightmare" street of film
8. Tennis legend Arthur
12. Perry with a Grammy and five Emmys
13. Aussie marsupial, slangily
14. Growth period
15. Neptune's spears
17. Butter alternative
18. Matt Damon is a NASA astronaut sent to an icy planet in this 2014 science fiction epic
20. Back muscle, in gym lingo
21. Fox's home
22. "Don't quit your day ___!"
25. Damon is a paroled car thief in another futuristic setting in this 2013 movie
28. "Ah, so sad"
30. Buck's belle
31. Camel feature
32. 2015 finds Damon in yet another science fiction story in "The ___ "

34. "Mad" or "Cosmo," e.g.
35. Very small
36. Dawdle
39. Damon is a European mercenary in this 2016 action monster film from China
44. "Old" British buddy
45. In ___ order (tidy)
46. Boone's nickname
47. Golf ball prop
48. "Blue" or "White" river
49. Fries or slaw, typically
50. "Slippery" swimmer
51. D.C. ball team, briefly

DOWN

1. "Macbeth" opener
2. Auto beeper
3. Do not include
4. Alpine holler
5. Young's partner in accounting
6. Former Mississippi Sen. Trent
7. Light German wine
8. Do away with
9. Sun parlor
10. A gardener, at times
11. Angsty music genre
16. ___ of Good Feelings, 1817–25
19. Deposit, as an egg
22. Ad-lib, musically

23. Ipanema greeting
24. What a shortstop may use to field a grounder
25. 1 billion years, in astronomy
26. "Pulp Fiction" actress Thurman
27. Automobile sticker fig.
29. Church bell spot
30. Certain hotel fee
33. Gerund ending
36. Boutonniere spot

37. Bermuda's ocean: abbr.
38. Oscar winner Edmund of "Miracle on 34th Street"
39. Asian cuisine choice
40. Alternative to saber or foil
41. Capital of Western Samoa
42. Bouncy tune
43. Cask dregs
44. Floppy successors

POP STARS

ACROSS

1. Little white lies
5. Improv routine
8. Allied jumping-off point of July 1944
12. Dust Bowl state: Abbr.
13. Big fuss
14. Aid for catching a mouse
15. Film critic
17. Bee, to Opie
18. Fred Astaire title role
20. "For ___ a jolly good fellow..."
21. "All's well," in space
22. Artifact from the past
25. African despot Amin
26. Play ___ with (make trouble for)
29. Apply frosting
30. Barbecue chef's wear
32. Track's governing org.
33. Baby's word
34. Gp. that sticks to their guns
35. Aisle with butter and eggs
37. Courtroom oath
38. Bygone nuclear agcy.
39. Little Orphan Annie's guardian
46. Berry plugged as a superfood

47. No-no at some intersections
48. "As I see it," online
49. ___ long (poetic "soon")
50. Assam silkworm
51. "Cheep" accommodations?
52. Angler's pole
53. Plaintiff's opposite: Abbr.

DOWN

1. Country legend Tennessee Ernie
2. Assemble-it-yourself furniture seller
3. Wide rd.
4. Gave an informal greeting
5. Cries loudly
6. Prefix for graph or logical
7. "The Wizard of Oz" weather event
8. Celery stem
9. "Can't argue with that"
10. "Auld ___ Syne"
11. Makes a choice
16. Head turner, say
19. Spend more than you have
22. Fix, as a horse race
23. "Green" opener
24. Author Tolstoy

152

25. "Deathtrap" author Levin
26. Yes, in Yokohama
27. Blade in the water
28. Act like a bull?
31. Sneak who's up to no good
36. More keen
37. "It is a tale told by an ___"

38. Barked, Sandy-style
39. Hammett's "The ___ Curse"
40. As high as you can go
41. Dashes in a code
42. Dynamic start?
43. Fix for what ails you
44. Actor-singer Kristofferson
45. Bean or dragon

ANSWERS ON PAGE 246.

LOOK ON THE BRIGHT SIDE

ACROSS

1. "Man, that's a relief!"
5. Subject of a 1773 protest
8. Boat ramp
12. "Drat!" is a mild one
13. Belief system
14. Bit of deception
15. "Cubist" Rubik
16. "7 Faces of Dr. ___" (Tony Randall pic)
17. Capital near fjords
18. Scintillating
21. Perfect to a gymnast
22. "Funeral in Berlin" author Deighton
23. Angry growl
25. It's not much
28. "Knot" homophone
30. Canada's neighbor, colloquially
33. Bogus
35. Letters in a URL
37. Boardroom attire
38. Instrument for the musically inept, maybe
40. "Mighty" tree
42. "Now do you believe me?"
43. Abysmal score
45. Actress Ullmann or Tyler
47. Campaigner, for short

49. Shining intensely
54. Disney's boy detective
56. Copy
57. "Parlez-___ francais?"
58. "Citizen ___" (Welles film)
59. Catnip mouse, for a cat
60. "___ Dinka Doo" (Jimmy Durante song)
61. "Cogito, ___ sum"
62. Language ending, sometimes
63. "Home on the Range" critter

DOWN

1. Bellyacher's litany
2. Dwell on tediously
3. 11,000-foot Italian peak
4. Fingerprint feature
5. To this moment
6. "NYPD Blue" star Morales
7. First ___ equals
8. "No more seats" sign
9. Gleaming
10. "Lord of the Flies" setting
11. Feudal drudge
19. "Jeopardy!" whiz Jennings
20. African antelope
24. Balaam's beast
25. Informal reproach

26. "Eureka!"
27. Eye-popping
29. Deuce
31. 'Bah!' relative
32. Absorbed the loss of
34. A brother of Curly
36. Large freshwater sport fish
39. Any planet, to a bard
41. About 5⁄8 of a mi.
44. Speechify

46. Intensely graphic
47. Chinese dog, for short
48. Rubaiyat maker
50. Nasdaq debuts
51. Tip-top
52. Cook in the microwave, slangily
53. Former Russian emperor
55. "The Lip" of baseball

ANSWERS ON PAGE 246.

IT'S IN YOUR HANDS

ACROSS

1. It's in your hands
5. Ice cream flavor, briefly
9. Audible dance
12. At leisure
13. Carrie on "The King of Queens"
14. A hot time, in Paris
15. Break ground
16. Lhasa ___
17. Coastal eagle
18. Man with a couch
20. Become frantic
22. Koop and Elders, for short
23. ___-Locka (town near Miami)
24. "Star Wars" genre
25. Having color
26. Immune system component
27. Patrick Stewart role
30. British bishops' hats
31. Time and ___ (overtime pay)
32. Saloon sounds
33. Polynesian wraparound skirt
34. Kind of battery: Abbr.
35. Relative of mdse.
38. Big occasion
39. Handel opus
41. Big foot spec
42. West Point initials
44. "The ___ Reader": eclectic magazine
45. French rifle range
46. "Walkabout" director Nicolas
47. "___ and the Detectives" (old Disney film)
48. "Roswell" regulars
49. Aer Lingus land
50. It's in your hands

DOWN

1. ___ a fiddle
2. Going too far, in a way
3. Earthen jars
4. "The Farmer in the ___"
5. Held tightly
6. Group of seven
7. Economic gp. formed in Bogota, 1948
8. They're in your hands
9. More microscopic
10. Not much at all
11. They're in your hands
19. It's in your hands
21. The FDIC may insure them
25. Guitarist Eddie Van ___
27. Tahiti's capital
28. "Here's the solution!"
29. They're in your hands
30. Odometer marking

156

32. It's in your hands
35. Cuban military base, for short
36. Zebra ___ (aquarium fish)
37. Beach find
40. Bird feeder cake
43. "___ sez to the guy..."

1	2	3	4		5	6	7	8		9	10	11
12					13					14		
15					16					17		
18				19				20	21			
22				23				24				
			25					26				
27	28	29					30					
31						32						
33						34				35	36	37
38						39		40				
41				42	43				44			
45				46					47			
48				49					50			

ANSWERS ON PAGE 247.

GUESS THE THEME

ACROSS

1. "Hey!" on the road
5. "Dombey and ___" (Dickens novel)
8. Amateur
12. All-purpose trucks
13. Brain of a PC
14. Basketball need
15. "Contrary" girl of rhyme
16. Ben-Hur was chained to one for three years
17. Hand-knotted rugs
18. Prevent entrance, in a way
21. Enjoying a win streak
22. Churchyard tree in "Romeo and Juliet"
23. Outdoor lounging spot
26. Many a hand sanitizer
27. "Death Becomes ___" (Meryl Streep film)
30. Shareholder's payment
33. Baby sitter's handful
34. Type of jet engine
35. Goes to the polls
36. "Slippery" fish
37. "___ lords a-leaping"
38. Hurdy-gurdy
43. Big cat of the Americas
44. Acorn source
45. Burglar's haul
47. Cupid counterpart
48. National monogram

49. Breaks up
50. Au pair's charge
51. "Honor ___ father"
52. Drip through an opening

DOWN

1. Borrow (forever)
2. "And a lot of others besides that," in four letters
3. Dulles designer Saarinen
4. Like a mind reader
5. "Patton" portrayer
6. Bright-colored fish
7. Dance great Rudolf
8. Kind of pillow or rug
9. Cello player Ma
10. "The Lion King" sound effect
11. Black ___ (covert doings)
19. More flaky
20. Bring to one's door, as mail
23. Air pressure letters
24. Bank convenience, for short
25. "___ Chef"
26. Card game or drink
27. All ___ up (agitated)
28. 180 degrees from WSW
29. Blvd. crossers

158

31. Distribute sparingly
32. Computer attachments
36. Do blackboard duty
37. Sweet Hungarian wine
38. Cover up
39. Crazed way to run
40. Batted body part, briefly
41. Top notch
42. Bump on a log, say
43. Dino, for the Flintstones
46. A bit more than a pinch: Abbr.

 ANSWERS ON PAGE 247.

MISNOMERS

ACROSS

1. Holy pilgrimage
5. Fireside chat pres.
8. Diva's big moment
12. A lightbulb can represent it
13. "Blame It on ___" (Michael Caine flick)
14. Club or baking follower
15. They aren't for parking and don't lead to parks
17. Junior in the NFL Hall of Fame
18. Confess, with "up"
19. Last word of "America the Beautiful"
21. They were invented by mathematicians in India
28. Bored, with "up"
29. 3, on sundials
30. Earth miniature
31. Aladdin's find
33. "Game, ___, match!"
35. Brit's subway
36. "Pong" company
38. Massage
40. "A mouse!"
41. They were so named for dogs, not birds
44. A pitcher wants a low one, for short
45. Pigeon call
46. Mine entrance
49. It's actually bright orange
54. Chore list topper
55. "___ voyage!"
56. Main river of Switzerland
57. Celestial hammerer
58. No specific one
59. A bit less than a meter

DOWN

1. "___ to Be Square" (Huey Lewis and the News hit)
2. Cavity-fighting org.
3. German "the"
4. Bob Dylan's youngest son
5. Drake the navigator
6. Abbr. for a handy-andy
7. "Martini and ___"
8. Battery partner
9. Fishy eggs
10. "Sweet" girl of songdom
11. Org. that sponsors the Junior Olympics
16. 1939-45 event, briefly
20. "Deviled" food
21. Company with a "spokesduck"
22. Calf catcher
23. Commercial creator
24. Celebrity chef Guy ___

160

25. Capital of Normandy
26. Died down
27. Is on the lookout for
32. Roman magistrate
34. Region whose capital is Florence
37. Discount clothing tag abbr.
39. Allied nations
42. Start of a "Flintstones" shout

43. Good to go
46. Big inits. in long distance
47. "Dumb, dumb, dumb!" to Homer Simpson
48. Affirmative at the altar
50. Actor Chaney, Jr.
51. Barnyard bleat
52. Bobby of hockey fame
53. Crossed (out)

ANSWERS ON PAGE 247.

FUN FADS

ACROSS

1. Part of FWIW
4. Corn eater's discards
8. Citrus drinks
12. Fifties fad involving undulation
14. Denim king Strauss
15. Heading uphill or downhill, e.g.
16. "Israel Through My Eyes" author
17. Backyard barbecue spot
18. Faddish '70s toy that came in a box with air holes
20. Bygone nuclear agcy.
22. "All By Myself" singer Celine
23. Boss of Hazzard County
26. Assists
28. Be in poor health
31. Poi base
32. "L'il ol' me?"
33. Be in accord with
34. Calypso offshoot
35. Capital of Western Samoa
36. Octopus octet
37. Action word
39. Barrister's field
41. Watch-Me-Grow fad

44. "Animal House" getups
48. Child's punishment, maybe
49. Legal escape hatch
51. Bonnie hillside
52. Trippy fad light of the '60s
53. "Mama" ___ Elliot
54. Paparazzi target
55. Amphibious carrier, for short

DOWN

1. "Rooty Tooty Fresh and Fruity" restaurant
2. Albacore or bluefin
3. Bedframe strip
4. Actress Sevigny
5. "Tic Tac Dough" win
6. Hale-___ comet
7. One-touch phone feature
8. 1999-2004 Olds model
9. Having a sophisticated charm
10. Emergency procedure, briefly
11. Kitchen necessity
13. Cheese similar to Parmesan
19. "My country ___ of thee"
21. Big name in soups

23. Abbr. after "Cleveland" or "Shaker"

24. "Tie a Yellow Ribbon" tree

25. High seriousness

27. Fever reading

29. "Big Blue" computer company

30. Bandleader Brown of renown

33. Aachen assent

35. Acclaimed Dadaist

38. Chalet overhangs

40. Equal to face value

41. Financial news network

42. Bar Mitzvah dance

43. Exactly as required

45. Kickstarter number

46. Charitable handouts

47. Fall mo.

50. Breakfast for Brutus, perhaps

ANSWERS ON PAGE 247.

THE NEXT BIG THING

ACROSS

1. Big, big, big
8. "___ la vista!"
13. Put in danger
14. "The Enemy Below" threat
15. Abraham's Oscar-winning role
16. Former Golden Arches burger
17. Greek letters
18. Big fuss
20. "Carte" or "mode" preceder
21. Big name in home dyes
22. "___ Tag" (German greeting)
23. 52, to Caesar
24. "___ Hard" (Willis film)
25. Most common family name in Vietnam
27. Colorado snowboarding mecca
30. Newspaper opinion pieces
31. He found the Pacific
33. French noble
34. A dozen eggs, in a lab
35. Branch, to a botanist
37. 180 degrees from NNW
40. Computer network acronym
41. "Just the facts, ___"

42. Low-lying wetland
43. Beginner's course
45. Juice brand owned by Coca-Cola
47. Impolite army acronym meaning "a big mess"
48. Like bankruptcy, maybe
49. Listens attentively
50. Mammoth

DOWN

1. Penny-pincher
2. Classic violin maker
3. Bug-on-the-windshield noise
4. Mexico City half-dozen
5. Angry emotion
6. Faith, hope, or charity
7. "Do I dare to eat a peach?" poet
8. Gigantic
9. "Jeopardy!" airer
10. Soap-making solution
11. Kept score
12. Gains through effort
19. Lion's hangout
22. Hyperbolically large
24. Ball gal
26. Bar code: Abbr.
27. Make illegal
28. Rhino's realm
29. Relating to the sole
32. 1.5-volt battery size

164

33. Soft-nosed bullet
36. Native New Zealander
37. Athenian law-giver
38. Stage direction that means "alone"
39. Backspace over text

42. A pride of lions?
44. Jack's Attorney General, initially
46. "Paris, Texas" director Wenders

ANSWERS ON PAGE 248.

HOLDING HANDS

ACROSS

1. Give for free, slangily
5. Caught in the rain
8. Bigger than big
12. Fiery gemstone
13. 1040 org.
14. About which the Earth turns
15. Abominable Snowman
16. Golf ball placement
17. Boring method to learn by
18. Fancy light fixtures holding a hand?
21. Busy buzzer
22. A doctrine or theory
23. Young turkey
26. Bout stoppers, briefly
27. Mom's month
30. Control, as lions
31. Activated, as a fuse
32. Apple throwaway
33. Jean of Dada
34. Classic name for a dinosaur
35. "Every ___ Way But Loose" (1978 film)
36. "Groovy!" relative
37. Amazement
38. Like drip-dry garments, holding a hand?
43. Add a bit of color to
44. "The Hunt for ___ October"
45. Duel provoker
47. A cappella range
48. Mine material
49. Architect Saarinen
50. Baby chick's sound
51. "Yes" gesture
52. Flow slowly

DOWN

1. Affectedly shy
2. 11-member cartel
3. Calculus, for example
4. Easily shaped
5. "The Importance of Being Earnest" author
6. One of the five Great Lakes
7. "Cats" poet
8. "Scheherazade" setting
9. Caesar's wife
10. Beats it, in the backwoods
11. Compass point opposite WSW
19. Butterfly catcher
20. Orbiting lab, for short
23. Sch. booster group
24. Rowboat need
25. Ballgame official
26. "Kid-tested, mother-approved" cereal
27. "Me?" to Miss Piggy

28. Rainbow path
29. "Uh-huh"
31. Classic Chrysler model
32. Brie and gouda
34. Cheer shout
35. Internet letters
36. Camera lens setting
37. Came up with a sum
38. Craftiness

39. A chip in the pot, perhaps
40. "Quo Vadis?" emperor
41. Safe, at sea
42. Like some stamps or steaks
43. "This Is Spinal ___"
46. Football coach Warner

1	2	3	4		5	6	7		8	9	10	11
12					13				14			
15					16				17			
	18			19				20				
			21				22					
23	24	25				26				27	28	29
30					31				32			
33				34				35				
		36				37						
	38	39				40				41	42	
43					44				45			46
47					48				49			
50					51				52			

ANSWERS ON PAGE 248.

ADVERTISING MASCOTS

ACROSS

1. Angler's buy
4. Quite a ways away
7. Goblet, for example
12. Sushi-bar soybean
14. Hall's musical partner
15. No longer working
16. An inedible orange
17. Former mascot for corn chips
19. New Jersey city at the eastern end of I-80
20. Small unit of force
23. Overhead light
24. Treehouse builder, often
27. Kennedy or Kerry of Massachusetts
29. Letter ender
31. "Live from New York!" initials
32. Old superpower
36. Christmas concert tune
37. Natural sugar
39. Spaghetti-in-a-can icon
44. Resident of a gulf state
45. Foolishness
46. Pop singer Lavigne
47. Split end
48. Che's chum
49. Fed. ID
50. Journal or Japan finish

DOWN

1. Maker of foam toys
2. Linda of Broadway's "Jekyll & Hyde"
3. Comedic filmmaker Jacques
4. Denmark's ___ Islands
5. One-celled organisms
6. Tiny biter
7. Pent-up emotion reliever
8. Eye surgery acronym
9. Rat- follower (gun sound)
10. Utah's state flower
11. Boston-to-Nantucket dir.
13. Hand holder?
18. USA's largest labor union
20. Platter spinners, for short
21. Hither's companion
22. Oiler's org.
24. Thelma and Louise, e.g.
25. Sendak's "Where the Wild Things ___ "
26. High-speed connection, briefly
28. Carry out
30. Like a close ball game
33. Aquatic vessel

34. Shows derision
35. Queens and princes
37. Aladdin associate
38. Chief evil
39. 906, in Roman numerals

40. Like diamonds
41. Netherlands sight
42. Summers in Europe
43. Jane in a Bronte title
44. Graceless sort

ANSWERS ON PAGE 248.

EVEN AS WE SPOCK

ACROSS

1. Series hosted by Leonard Nimoy
6. Was humbled
7. Up and about
9. Underworld river
10. Sci-fi series in which Nimoy played Spock
12. Beach near Omaha
13. Postseason gridiron game
18. Start of a catch phrase of Spock
20. Blue green shade
22. Get-acquainted event
23. Statement of surrender
24. End of the catch phrase

DOWN

1. Playful words to a toddler
2. Comedy routine
3. Highly perceptive
4. Cyberspace place
5. How the elated walk
6. As well
8. Lodge members
11. Postal receptacle
14. After-dinner drink
15. Chowder choice
16. Deep blue
17. Access for a wheelchair
19. One of Santa's reindeer
21. Barely noticeable amount

ANSWERS ON PAGE 248.

THE AMERICANS

ACROSS

1. Philip portrayer in Joe Weisberg's "The Americans"
8. Blush
9. Latin dance
10. "To A Skylark," e.g.
11. "Do whatever you want"
13. Espionage novel by Joe Weisberg, who created "The Americans"
16. Prove to be competent
19. "Sure thing"
21. One way to cook clams
22. Be unfaithful to
23. Elizabeth portrayer in Joe Weisberg's "The Americans"

DOWN

1. D.C. subway
2. Hit man
3. "Ready or not, ___ come"
4. Roll of bills
5. Exercise wheel runner
6. "Lion King" cub
7. Foxworthy's field
12. Pound part
13. "Close, but no cigar!"
14. Ringo, for one
15. Do a free fall
17. Smart ___
18. Blizzard equipment
20. Bloodhound's clue
22. Adhesive for feathers

ANSWERS ON PAGE 249.

HIDDEN CLUE

ACROSS

1. Fleeting success
8. Asian archipelago
9. Bench press target
10. Light haircut
11. Large amphibian
14. Characteristic of a Type A
16. Excuse designed to elicit tears
18. Spoiled kid
21. Neither's companion
22. Middleman
24. Saver of nine

DOWN

1. Act the coquette
2. Confusing
3. Word for "clue" hidden in the three long answers
4. Denials
5. Without deliberation
6. Hamelin's rat catcher, for one
7. Last place finisher, proverbially
12. Absolute
13. "Don't go anywhere!"
14. Shout of praise
15. Haifa inhabitant
17. Military cap
19. Subtle coloration
20. Nonlethal phaser setting
23. Expression of disdain

ANSWERS ON PAGE 249.

MAHERSHALA ALI MOVIES

ACROSS

1. Auto's wheel bar
5. Xfinity, e.g.: abbr.
8. All-encompassing phrase
12. Balance bar
13. "Me day" destination
14. "Without You" band Mötley ___
15. Advocate strongly
16. Big name in physics
18. Ali was world-class pianist Dr. Don Shirley in this 2018 film
20. A false god
21. 1921 Karel Capek play that introduced the word "robot"
22. Vermont music festival town
25. Health ins. plan
28. Ali was military officer Jim Johnson in this 2016 hit
31. Add-___ (extras)
32. State of inactivity
33. A word from Elsie
35. Prefix meaning eight
36. Ali was Juan, a drug dealer, in this 2016 movie
39. Assumed to be true
41. Gets ready to shoot

44. "I saw ___ kissing Kate..." (tongue twister)
45. "Dune" composer Brian
46. Dubious
47. Biweekly tide
48. "Do not open ___ Xmas"
49. Long-distance swimmer Diana

DOWN

1. Aladdin's monkey
2. Baby Boomer's kid
3. Slowpokes
4. Green gem
5. "Ah, got it"
6. Bit of public relations deception
7. Cook uncovered with no fat
8. Mahershala Ali, for one
9. "Star ___" (Shatner show)
10. "Most assuredly, monsieur!"
11. Branch of Buddhism
17. Coin of little value
19. River through Germany
20. Actor Conrad or actress Barbara
22. Electrical unit now known as a siemens
23. Small planted bulb

176

24. "Mayberry ___" (old TV show)
25. Make attractive
26. Bit of "dinero"
27. CIA forerunner
29. Mapmaker's subj.
30. Remove shackles
33. Clean the deck
34. Tic-tac-toe win
36. Assigner of G's and R's

37. German director Riefenstahl
38. "Survivor" immunity item
39. China's Sun Yat-___
40. What scuff marks show
42. Advanced music or drama deg.
43. "Danny and the Dinosaur" author ___ Hoff

ANSWERS ON PAGE 249.

GOOD-BYE, GOOD BUY

ACROSS

1. Good buy
9. Bargain-priced
10. Publicly criticize
11. Evaluated
12. A burning desire?
13. Good-bye
15. Ancient empire of Asia
18. Room at the top
20. Good buy
23. Bing Crosby, for one
24. Olympics award
25. Good-bye

DOWN

2. Twisted treat
3. Matchmaker with wings
4. Endure without protest
5. Off with permission
6. Adult polliwogs
7. Building with a dome
8. "Bullets" in poker
13. Ouija board meetings
14. "Sorry, that's not possible!"
16. Stunt double, for one
17. Spain plus Portugal
19. Hidden treasure
21. Shakespearean loverboy
22. Cairo river

ANSWERS ON PAGE 249.

JOHN GOTTI

ACROSS

1. Airport boarding area
5. One of Gotti's nicknames was "___ Don"
11. Difficult skating jump
12. Court crier's words
13. Get a new loan, slangily
14. Had a debate
15. Big initials in fashion
16. Annual stage award since 1956
17. "Good Vibrations" or "Surfin' Safari"
19. C.S.A. soldier
22. Assembly of church officials
24. Far from fresh
26. Final musical passage
27. As high as you can get
28. Tag ___ with (accompany)
30. Big name in cameras
31. Day of many a Fed. holiday
32. Familiar fruit logo
34. Aspersion
35. Golf peg
38. Obi Wan, to Luke
41. Breakfast or lunch
42. Nicholson's threesome
43. It's more, in a saying
44. Baby's knitwear
45. La ___ Tar Pits

DOWN

1. Cooper of "High Noon"
2. Cabin builders' need
3. After three acquittals, Gotti came to be known as the ___
4. Yale grad
5. Oil emirate Abu ___
6. Eagles' nests
7. Book leaf
8. Boston skyscraper, informally, with "the"
9. Daisy center
10. Crimson or scarlet
16. Curious
18. Advance from a shark
19. Capone, e.g., or Gotti
20. "Sesame Street" ticklee
21. Existed
22. A Ponzi scheme is one
23. Texter's "carpe diem"
25. Suspect's shadow
29. Aplenty
30. "All Things Considered" carrier
33. Change holder
34. Now, in the ICU
36. Comfortable situation
37. "Frozen" belle
38. Capo's crowd
39. "___ Beso" ("That Kiss," Anka hit)

40. Drill sgt. e.g.

41. Org. for the Boys of Summer

ANSWERS ON PAGE 250.

HOW TO TAKE CHARGE

ACROSS

1. "A Fish Called ___"
6. Frozen drip
12. Kill the exam, slangily
13. Pay a visit to
14. Take charge in the henhouse?
16. Base eatery
17. Golf course peg
18. Have a bite
19. Electric-fan sound
20. Take charge at the immunization clinic?
25. Harem rooms
26. Brit's bathroom
27. Cambodian leader Lon ___
28. Old-fashioned letter opener
33. Take charge in a horse race?
35. Capital of Montana
36. "The Destroyer," in Hinduism
37. Some mattresses
38. Carved Native American pole

DOWN

1. Less than hot
2. Missed ___: blew one's entrance
3. "Little House on the Prairie" character ___ Oleson
4. Many truck engines
5. To boot
6. Bjork's country: abbr.
7. Poet Sandburg
8. UN agcy. that won the 1969 Nobel Peace Prize
9. Fate who spins the thread of life
10. Come unglued
11. Comes in
15. "What ___ God wrought"
19. Directory of notables
20. Spiral shells
21. Old-time actress Renee
22. Fingers-in-ears sounds
23. "In the Valley of ___" (2007 Tommy Lee Jones film)
24. Like the worst loser
28. Big Apple fashion inits.
29. Airport arr. estimates
30. "___ the jackpot!"
31. Paris's ___ Gauche
32. Unsolicited e-mail
34. Disney film frame

ANSWERS ON PAGE 250.

HOME AT LAST

ACROSS

1. Not none but not all
5. Make a swap
10. Go ___ length (ramble)
11. Felt below par
12. Note-taker's need
14. Stress reliever
15. Sacred
16. Texter's "Didn't need to know that"
17. "Welcome" rug
19. Phantom's home
24. Grp. that entertains troops
25. The Silver State: abbr.
26. RR stops
29. Bangor's state
31. Money-saving investment
33. "Au revoir!"
34. Offshoot group
35. Have a bite of
36. Topkapi palace chambers

DOWN

1. South African uprising site
2. Entrance to a freeway
3. "Game of Thrones" actress Williams
4. Suffix for kitchen or luncheon
5. "Joy Luck Club" author
6. Brit's "Sure thing!"
7. Big name in pet food
8. Negotiation goal
9. Swirl of water
13. Rombauer and La Douce
18. What the last word at 12-, 19-, and 31-Across can be
20. Dark brown potato
21. JetBlue rival
22. "What fools these mortals be" writer
23. Tennis great Chris and family
26. Bit of baseball card info
27. "And there you have it!"
28. Center of rotation
30. Furthermore
32. Shade of color

ANSWERS ON PAGE 250.

GETTING GOOSEBUMPS

ACROSS

1. Alley prowler
4. Quiz bowl fodder
10. "Bravo!" kin
11. Hero of a Virgil epic
12. R.L. Stine book about creepy-crawlies
14. Text message command
15. De Niro's Manhattan restaurant
16. Crime-lab material
19. Managua is its cap.
20. R.L. Stine book about a spooky cave at the shore
24. Go jogging
25. That lady
26. U.S. citizen: abbr.
28. Like a loafer
32. R.L. Stine book about an evil rabbit
35. Actress Lansbury or Bassett
36. Terrific tennis shot
37. Start a round of golf
38. Positive response

DOWN

1. Gear teeth
2. Healing balm
3. New driver, usually
4. Skin art, for short
5. VCR's "Go back"
6. Privy to, as a joke
7. "Romeo and Juliet" town
8. Like Shakespeare's sonnets
9. In itself
13. Sums up
17. To the ___ degree (extremely)
18. Teddy's Mt. Rushmore neighbor
20. Try to snatch
21. Showing compassion
22. Ill at ease
23. View from Cleveland
27. Word form meaning "current"
29. 1944 Normandy landing
30. Doily material
31. Mr. Potato Head parts
33. Furry sitcom alien
34. Brit. fliers

ANSWERS ON PAGE 250.

FUNKY FASHION

ACROSS

1. Alliance agreement
5. Bivouacs
10. Famous ___ (cookie brand)
11. "La ___" (opera house)
12. Quirky topper worn by Buster Keaton, Fozzie Bear, and Rocky Balboa
14. Alpine ridge
15. ___-Flush (bathroom cleaner)
16. Place to get a mud bath
18. British author Deighton
19. High-heeled custom footwear for drag queens in a book, movie, and play
23. Ending for prop- or meth-
24. Clump of turf
25. St. John's is its capital: abbr.
27. Campus brass
31. Lolita-type playsuits of skirts with bib and straps
33. Asian cartoon genre

34. Breach of contract, for example
35. Hard to climb, perhaps
36. Mil. addresses

DOWN

1. He "loves mambo"
2. Cherub with a bow
3. Apple center
4. Tongue-clucking sounds
5. CBS forensic franchise
6. Sampras sizzlers
7. "Thanks," at a luau
8. Metropolis paper
9. Lustrous fabrics
13. 17th century diarist Samuel
17. "Humble" dwelling place
19. Sunflower State
20. Crib occupant
21. Soprano Melba
22. One-named singer from Alabama
26. Capitol crown
28. On the highest point
29. "Fiddler" of old Rome
30. Fast fliers of yore: abbr.
32. Kind of rally or talk

FAVE FLAVES

ACROSS

1. Get cleaned up
5. Hotel quotes
10. Prefix meaning "Mars"
11. "Oh give me ___, where the..."
12. Object on many a kitchen table
14. Oro y ___ (Montana's motto)
15. Actress Spelling
16. Foot soldiers: abbr.
18. Colorado creek
19. Object on many a kitchen table
23. Cornhusker's sch.
24. "The Serpent and the Rope" novelist Raja
25. Aspiring atty.'s exam
27. Mystery writer Marsh
31. Objects on many a kitchen table
33. Resort isle off Venezuela
34. London lavs
35. "Touched By an Angel" star Della
36. District near Piccadilly

DOWN

1. Builder of paper nests
2. Dwindling Asian sea
3. Ward of "House, M.D."
4. Tout's tidbit
5. College cheer
6. At the drop of ___ (immediately)
7. Michener's "The Bridges at ___"
8. "Bam!" man in the kitchen
9. Cliffhanger genre
13. Having more marbles?
17. Former French coin
19. Neutron star
20. Make certain (that)
21. One of ten in Exodus
22. Ski-slope bumps
26. Bar bills
28. Peek-___ (baby's game)
29. The "I" in I. M. Pei
30. ___ buco (veal dish)
32. Actress Charlotte of "The Facts of Life"

ANSWERS ON PAGE 251.

FAIR SHARES?

ACROSS

1. Fourth Estate
6. ___ Na Na ("Grease" group)
9. Like some Coast Guard rescues
11. Arctic area: abbr.
12. Spouse, jokingly
14. Bar orders
15. Lily with arrow-shaped leaves
16. Less difficult
17. Game division
21. On a "What's Hot" list
22. Mystery writer Gardner et al.
23. Churchill prop
27. Start some origami, perhaps
29. Angelico or Diavolo
30. Sun Tzu's "___ of War"
31. Mt. Carmel locale
32. Fast horses

DOWN

1. Onetime sunblock agent
2. Cambodian coin
3. Art Deco painter
4. Booming jets of old
5. Call at poker
6. Supreme Court conservative
7. Scholar who wrote "If not now, when?"
8. Sandy sounds
10. In literature, a peaceful place
13. Corned beef dish
16. Finishes, as a relationship
17. Graf on the court
18. Blunders
19. Wine locale, often
20. Like a line, briefly
23. She had a show with Sonny
24. Tiny battery size
25. Strike-monitoring org.
26. Immature newts
28. New Deal home loan gp.

ANSWERS ON PAGE 251.

DUBIOUS DEFINITIONS

ACROSS

1. Short profile
4. Civil rights grp. since 1909
9. Incoming flight: abbr.
10. Canadian physician Sir William ___
11. Unwrite, as a symphony?
13. He sold out to Jacob
14. Beret cousin
15. Cassiterite or stannite
18. Took off one's Jockey shorts?
21. Take into custody
22. Peeples or Vardalos
23. Spanish hors d'oeuvre
27. Taking back the food?
30. Big name in printers
31. Casino cube
32. Like a starfish
33. T or F, on exams

DOWN

1. Said, as farewell
2. Causes wrath
3. "Free Willy" animal
4. ___ de plume (pen name)
5. Egyptian serpent
6. Many
7. Lucrezia Borgia's brother
8. Aspiring doc's program
12. Beyond unconventional
16. Sue Grafton's "___ for Innocent"
17. Hulu or Ustream, e.g.
18. Get one's ___ up: get angry
19. City down the shore from Buffalo, N.Y.
20. Like trumpet music
24. Operatic slave girl
25. Nabokov's title professor
26. Gets on in years
28. Fair-hiring inits.
29. Three-min. period, in the ring

1	2	3	■	4	5	6	7	8
9			■	10				
11			12					
13				■		14		
■	■	■	15	16	17			
18	19	20						
21						■	■	■
22			■	■	23	24	25	26
27			28	29				
30					■	31		
32					■	33		

ANSWERS ON PAGE 251.

KNIVES OUT

ACROSS

1. Pretty-picture link
4. Many a soccer rooter
7. Emphatic ending with yes or no
12. Character of a fabric
14. Pretzels, basically
15. Sparks
16. Lofty objective
17. He was Benoit Blanc in "Knives Out"
19. Classic Buick
20. Banana castoff
23. Nobel-winning author Wiesel
24. Canon camera model
27. Riverbank word in "American Pie" lyrics
29. God, in the Quran
31. Cheer for the matador
32. Sunscreen compound
36. Full of uncertainties
37. Small taxi
39. Oscar category that Ana de Armas was nominated for
43. Salon overhaul
45. Sun parlors
46. Kilt pattern
47. Blackboard chore
48. Rolls's partner
49. License to drill, for short?
50. ___ out: scrape by

DOWN

1. Not much at all
2. Will be, in a 1956 hit song
3. Nerve impulse carrier
4. What the Louvre is, to a Parisian
5. Ultimatum words
6. Agave drink
7. Winter sports mecca
8. Sundance entry
9. "Walkabout" director Nicolas
10. JFK posting
11. Subj. for some bilinguals
13. Armor plate for the thigh
18. Cleanup hitter's goal, briefly
20. Old Mideast org.
21. Long-bodied swimmer
22. "Killing ___" (Sandra Oh spy drama)
24. Gnome cousin
25. Lumbering sort
26. Not forthcoming
28. Series unit
30. Many October babies

33. Morsel for a toad
34. Unfit to judge
35. Diplomatic agreement
37. Battlefield doc
38. Titan who holds up the heavens

39. NYC theater district
40. Lake by Ontario
41. Kitchen fixture
42. Wizard
43. "Tell Me More" network
44. "Mr. Blue Sky" band

ANSWERS ON PAGE 252.

DOOHICKEYS

ACROSS

1. Utah city named for a Biblical kingdom
5. Precious stone weight
10. He loved an Irish Rose
11. Tropical hat
12. Gizmo
14. Hard to catch
15. Opposite of sml.
16. What two heads are better than
17. Suffix for "arbor" or "ether"
18. Doodad
23. Brain scan, briefly
24. Campers, for short
25. "Volare (___ blu di pinto di blu)"
26. Big-beaked tropical birds
30. Whatchamacallit
32. Epic Virgil poem
33. Go on a tirade
34. Words before golf clubs or silverware
35. Madrid ladies: abbr.

DOWN

1. Chemical spray
2. Ancient Greek coin
3. Aborigine of Japan
4. Plays, as a horse
5. Matador's prop
6. Picnic intruder
7. Complained loudly
8. Ethically challenged
9. Hair snarl
11. It has a hard smooth surface
13. Bilbo Baggins's find
18. Dressed like
19. Tittering sound
20. Like a crystal chandelier
21. Egg cell
22. Film trophies
26. End-of-week initials
27. Slightly open
28. Name hidden in Hirschfeld caricatures
29. Army NCOs
31. Hero of "The Matrix"

ANSWERS ON PAGE 252.

TRUE DETECTIVE

ACROSS

1. Blue suit fabric
6. Copy playfully
11. Author Lafcadio ___
12. At a smart clip
13. Like a rainbow
14. Some salmons
15. "I am such a dummy!"
16. Dream Team letters
18. "Lord of the Rings" tree creature
19. Invest with authority
22. Like a library book
24. "The Thin Man" dog
27. Offer a carrot to, say
28. Ghostly pale
29. Gospel singer Winans
30. Neighbor of Brazil
31. Endocrine gland
33. Repetitive behavior condition, for short
35. Billing fig.
36. US Army in Europe
39. Color whose name comes from the Persian word for "dust"
41. Brassy blast
43. Japanese noodles
44. Immigrants' island in New York Harbor
45. Analyze, as metal
46. Decree from the king

DOWN

1. Fish similar to a herring
2. Architect Saarinen
3. She is Detective "Ani" Bezzerides in Season 2
4. Ph.D. seeker's exam
5. Reach, eventually
6. Colorful parrot
7. Dot-com's debut
8. He is Detective Wayne Hays in Season 3
9. Computer program symbol
10. "___ Si Bon" (1950s Eartha Kitt hit)
17. Heir, often
20. Bicycle with an engine
21. Gut course
22. Available without an Rx
23. "Born," in wedding notices
25. "Down for the count" count
26. Santa ___ (Pacific wind)
28. Opie Taylor's caretaker
30. Onyx or opal
32. Save for a ___ day
33. Creole vegetable
34. Cartoonist Addams, for short
37. "I Shot the Sheriff" singer Clapton
38. Big whoop-de-do

40. Hawaii's highest peak, Mauna ___

42. Atty.'s degree

1	2	3	4	5		6	7	8	9	10
11						12				
13						14				
15				16	17			18		
	19	20				21				
22	23						24		25	26
27						28				
29					30					
	31		32							
33	34			35				36	37	38
39			40			41	42			
43						44				
45						46				

ANSWERS ON PAGE 252.

AMERICAN SERIAL KILLERS

ACROSS

1. Goblet, e.g.
6. Eye rudely
11. Record-company name
12. "No more procrastinating!"
13. Sports venue
14. Fully up-to-date
15. Rodney Alcala was called the "___ ___ Killer" because he appeared on the game show in the midst of his killing spree
17. Playful river critter
18. Early stage of life
21. A bit wet
25. Fan's rebuke
26. Grumpy colleague?
27. Dinghy or canoe
29. "___ Fables"
32. Kind of bird or riser
34. John Norman Collins was known as the "___ ___"
39. Japanese meal in a box
40. Like sheep
41. Beneath, in Berlin
42. Country star Tucker
43. Brick-and-mortar operation
44. "Slammin' Sammy" of golf

DOWN

1. Happy or content
2. "Doctor Zhivago" heroine
3. Act as a lookout, e.g.
4. Graduate-to-be
5. Like italic type
6. Performer's platform
7. In the direction of
8. Eden evacuee
9. Almost never seen
10. Hole in a needle
16. '60s Pontiac muscle car
18. Flow out
19. "Got milk?" comeback, perhaps
20. Anaconda's cousin
22. Fuss and feathers
23. Hard-to-comb hair
24. Many computers
28. Balance unsteadily
29. Floating biblical sanctuary
30. George and T.S.
31. Very wooded
33. Go gaga over
34. It won't buy much
35. Fully aware of
36. Fishing cord
37. "A Day Without Rain" singer

38. Enjoy a magazine

39. Clear tables and such

ANSWERS ON PAGE 252.

DIET CONSCIOUS

ACROSS

1. Autobahn auto
4. Beer bottle top
7. Diet with an intake of certain liquids
12. Equinox month: abbr.
13. Flamenco yell
14. Knotted scarf
15. Add-on for Gator
16. Round object that can be eaten on a 55-Across diet
17. Perhaps
18. Big name in weight loss and diet programs
21. "Be there in just ____!"
22. Bug's antenna
26. Vietnam's capital
29. Nest egg inits.
30. Diet inspired by eating patterns around a European sea
35. "Let's call ____ night"
36. Doglike scavenger
37. Hollywood's Hedy
40. Song spelled with arm motions
43. Diet named for a Miami locale
47. Finds fault
50. Kia model
51. Wine and dine
52. Beaded counters of old

53. Wrap up
54. Bobble the ball, e.g.
55. Diet without animal consumption
56. Messy place
57. "CSI" evidence": abbr.

DOWN

1. Key of Brahms's Piano Trio No. 1 : abbr.
2. Movie matriarch played by Tyler Perry
3. Small songbirds
4. Imitator
5. One of the Baldwin brothers
6. Tree for a partridge in song
7. Oscar winner Foxx for "Ray"
8. Gas bill info
9. Wintry
10. Kernel holder
11. Summer on the Seine
19. Grape soda brand
20. Blazing
23. Commit perjury
24. Laundry brand
25. Bled in the wash
27. Jacket named for an Indian leader
28. Suffix of direct or transit

30. "Cool" amount at a heist
31. Greek H
32. River blocker
33. "Is ____ there?"
34. Christen
38. U.S. pet protector: abbr.
39. Violin bow application
41. Imitated a crow

42. Oak-to-be
44. "____ bien!" : Fr.
45. Subtle help
46. Celebratory dance
47. Cleveland NBAer, for short
48. Bearded president, for short
49. Dust cloth

ANSWERS ON PAGE 253.

SHERLOCK

ACROSS

1. Canvas cover?
6. "The March King" John Philip ___
11. Comforter
12. Arm bones
13. Benedict ___ is Holmes in "Sherlock"
15. Remarked
16. Angry feeling
17. Mrs. Hudson is played by ___ Stubbs
20. Lincoln's debate opponent
22. Gallup, Harris or Roper
24. Comic strip lightbulb
25. The E of HOMES
29. Assign to an obscure place
33. Act of deliberate betrayal
36. Big initials in fashion
37. "Awesome!" in the '80s
38. Kennedy and Danson
40. He plays criminal mastermind Jim Moriarty in "Sherlock"
45. "Murder, She Wrote" setting
46. Where Ephesus was located
47. Boiling pot's output
48. Short online posting

DOWN

1. Chest muscle, for short
2. Sports org. for nonprofessionals
3. Political doctrine
4. Birds' beaks
5. Sneaker patterns
6. Bring under control
7. Commercial ending for Cray- or Motor
8. No later than
9. Pelvic bones
10. Volcanic residue
14. One who really makes you laugh
17. AP rival, once
18. Agree wordlessly
19. Pint in a pub
21. Rupert Graves plays DI ___ Lestrade
23. Irene Adler, "The Woman," is played by ___ Pulver in "Sherlock"
26. "The Martian Chronicles" author Bradbury
27. Manilow's "___ a Miracle"
28. Slippery swimmer
30. Hold in regard
31. M-G-M co-founder Marcus

32. Breaks up a relationship
33. Aerial railway cars
34. Charged, as a bull
35. Funny Murphy
39. Trash-hauling boat

41. Cell "messenger," briefly
42. Number that's its own square root
43. All-even score
44. Work at lace-making

1	2	3	4	5		6	7	8	9	10
11						12				
13					14					
			15					16		
17	18	19		20			21			
22			23							
24							25	26	27	28
			29	30	31	32				
33	34	35						36		
37				38			39			
40			41					42	43	44
45						46				
47						48				

ANSWERS ON PAGE 253.

FASHION FORWARD

ACROSS

1. Wide-eyed predators
5. Lincoln and Burrows
9. Old hand, for short
12. Violent public disorder
13. Guy
14. Lamb's mother
15. Fashion designer Liz
17. Movie critic Reed
18. Confuse
19. Aviator Amelia
21. Exile isle for Napoleon
23. Tool with teeth
24. Bother persistently
27. Sightseeing trip
29. Nukes
32. Insubstantial
34. Golfer Sandra with 42 LPGA Tour wins, 1962-1982
36. In person
37. Hauled into court
39. Comprehend
40. Sense organ
42. Manicurist's focus
44. Michigan city
47. Relieves
51. "Monsters, _____"
52. Fashion designer Yves
54. To the _____ degree
55. Fast-food magnate Ray
56. Strip in the Middle East
57. Tofu source

58. Seasoning herb
59. School in England

DOWN

1. Killer whale
2. Rampant
3. Laundry unit
4. Subway entrance
5. Hubbub
6. Dresser
7. "Giant" writer Ferber
8. Prophets
9. Fashion designer known for her wedding gowns
10. Ornamental jug
11. Schoolbook
16. Trouser accessories
20. Obscured by air pollution
22. "_____ on the Side" (Whoopi Goldberg film)
24. Org. of Lions and Bears
25. The Greatest
26. Fashion designer Hubert de _____
28. Perlman of "Cheers"
30. Pizza order
31. Matched group
33. Butcher's offering
35. French farewell
38. Clear a drain
41. Jeopardizes
43. Big

44. Brooches
45. Not taken in by
46. Gillette blade
48. Part of pants
49. Automaker Ferrari
50. Spider-Man creator Lee
53. High card

ANSWERS ON PAGE 253.

LEADING AMYS

ACROSS

1. Tread heavily
6. Laura Bush's alma mater: abbr.
9. Completely
12. Peter of "The Maltese Falcon"
13. Beer container
14. Actress Farrow
15. "Yentl" costar
17. Up until now
18. County singer Williams or Ritter
19. Neill or Nunn
20. Bicker
22. Be the right size
23. Part of ACLU: abbr.
24. Singing syllables
27. Disentangle
30. Peruvian capital
31. The theme of this puzzle
32. Med student's subject: abbr.
33. Islands near Jamaica
35. Mink's playful cousin
36. Up to the job
37. Place for a mud bath
38. West Point student
40. Meadow
41. Mining excavation
44. Nest-egg investment option: abbr.

45. She played Dr. Coburn on "ER"
48. Director Burton
49. Christianity or Buddhism: abbr.
50. Loan-sharking
51. Harris and O'Neill
52. Sault _____ Marie: abbr.
53. Relaxes

DOWN

1. Shutter or blind part
2. Scholarly volume
3. Gemsbok
4. Medical imaging: abbr.
5. Iran, pre-1935
6. Milk choice
7. Restroom sign
8. Entertainer Leslie
9. Wife of Vince Gill
10. In _____ of
11. Tardy
16. Industrial container
21. Soprano Tebaldi
22. Set food on fire
23. Whatever
24. Mom's offering: abbr.
25. Long, narrow inlet
26. "Julie & Julia" costar
27. Hesitation sounds
28. "Norma _____" (1979 Sally Field film)
29. Photocopier option: abbr.

210

31. Sue _____ Langdon
34. Temple tables
35. Without luster
37. The Mediterranean, e.g.
38. Make reference to
39. Like Death Valley
40. Singer Lovett
41. Name of 12 popes
42. Memo opening
43. "_____ in the Attic"
46. Ran into
47. U.N. host: abbr.

ANSWERS ON PAGE 253.

ADAM DRIVER FILMS

ACROSS

1. "Pirates of the Caribbean" series star
5. "Aladdin" prince
8. A/C rating units
12. "Adios," in Italy
13. "Mad Men" actor Hamm
14. ___ buco (veal dish)
15. About, in contracts
16. "Just do it" or "Got milk?"
18. Adam Driver was FBI agent Daniel Jones in this 2019 political drama
20. Animation frames
21. "Isn't that cute?" sounds
22. Like a needle or a nut
25. "The Color of Money" prop
28. Driver played stage director Charlie Barber in this 2019 movie with Scarlett Johansson
31. Hoppin' mad feeling
32. Zinfandel, e.g.
33. Biblical floating zoo
35. A long, long time
36. Driver was Lev Shapiro in this 2012 film with Greta Gerwig

39. "Evidently!"
41. "Clown of the orchestra"
44. Modern encyclopedia platform
45. "Blueberries for ___" (classic children's book)
46. Arm bone
47. Arch molding
48. "Tinker, Tailor, Soldier, ___"
49. Be at ease

DOWN

1. 601, in old Rome
2. "A" in German class
3. Ornamental garden or theater section
4. Comic actress Amy
5. "When is a door not a door? When it's ___"
6. Bonanza vein
7. To a great degree
8. Churlish chaps
9. Air Force NCO
10. Chant at the Olympics
11. "Dombey and ___" (Dickens)
17. Gear for going up hills
19. Actor Morales of "Paid in Full"
20. Arctic trout
22. "Don't need those details!"

212

23. Conrad's "Heart of ___"
24. "It's all about me" trait
25. Like silver and gold
26. Banquet coffeepots
27. "Good ___!" (praise for a batter)
29. Keeps company with
30. Like some parking
33. Beloved PGA nickname
34. "King ___" (James Clavell novel)
36. Not bona fide
37. Be a good fan
38. Jed Clampett's daughter
39. "Letters From ___ Jima": 2006 film
40. Bummed smoke
42. Carry-___ (some luggage)
43. "All you can ___" (buffet sign)

ANSWERS ON PAGE 254.

WOMEN OF ACTION

ACROSS

1. "Lara Croft: _____ Raider" (2001 movie)
5. Air-gun ammo
8. Burlap fiber
12. 1998 Sarah McLachlan hit
13. Remy in "Ratatouille"
14. Right after
15. Mardi Gras follower
16. Singer Midge
17. Adriatic resort
18. CBS drama series
21. Mandela's organization: abbr.
22. Golf ball position
23. Captain of cereal
26. Accumulate interest
30. Travel in cyberspace
31. Bicorn and tricorn
32. Block houses?
35. Meryl in "Julie & Julia"
37. "His Master's Voice" company: abbr.
38. Polynesian dish
39. Star of 18-Across
46. Regal name of Norway
47. Caviar
48. Scrabble piece
49. Birthmark
50. Favorite Favre target
51. Brainstorm
52. Look through a keyhole

53. _____ Paulo
54. Gave the once-over

DOWN

1. After-shower application
2. River to the Baltic
3. Skirt length
4. 1995 Jim Carrey film
5. Midmorning meal
6. Theda "The Vamp"
7. "A Streetcar Named Desire" role
8. "Doctor Zhivago" star
9. "Wrapped _____ You": Garth Brooks song
10. Sarah Palin's hubby
11. "Dukes of Hazzard" spinoff
19. "Monsters, _____" (2001 animated film)
20. Karaoke need, briefly
23. CBS forensic drama
24. Trapdoor concealer
25. Internet address
27. Charlotte of "The Facts of Life"
28. SUV, for short
29. Psychic's skills: abbr.
33. Witch month: abbr.
34. Buffalo wings?
35. Michael Phelps sponsor
36. Taos lift

39. Ceremonial display
40. Skin-cream additive
41. Wind of 49-50 knots
42. Gossip queen Barrett

43. Spick-and-span
44. General Robert _____
45. Pick up a book

1	2	3	4		5	6	7		8	9	10	11
12					13				14			
15					16				17			
18				19				20				
			21				22					
23	24	25					26			27	28	29
30									31			
32				33	34		35	36				
			37				38					
39	40	41				42				43	44	45
46					47				48			
49					50				51			
52					53				54			

ANSWERS ON PAGE 254.

HAWAII FIVE-O

ACROSS

1. Coin opening
5. Joint chief?
11. Modern acronym suggesting "seize the day"
12. "Lawrence of Arabia" star Peter
13. Chow time, for many
14. Sherwood or Arden
15. Flightless bird of Australia
16. Quite a few
17. Prepare Parmesan, say
19. Former Atl. crosser
22. Dislike, and then some
24. Excellent or boffo, in "Variety"
26. Dance sometimes seen on "Hawaii Five-0"
27. Cut of pork
28. Breezing through, as an exam
30. Insignificant
31. Good, in France
32. Fancy tie
34. Commando rifles
35. Cornfield call
38. Christmas tree strands
41. Officer Tani Rey is played by Meaghan ___
42. One-cell creature
43. Longest Swiss river

44. Museum busts
45. Annoying flier

DOWN

1. "Auld Lang___"
2. Weaver's device
3. Alex who plays Steve McGarrett
4. Heavy weight
5. McGarrett's longtime nemesis
6. Makes amends for
7. "Gilmore Girls" girl
8. John or Bambi
9. Ernie on the links
10. Trapeze artist's need
16. Damage slightly
18. Chestnut horse
19. He plays "Danno" Williams
20. Revue component
21. Kellogg's tiger
22. "Moby Dick" whaler
23. Osso ___ (veal dish)
25. Butter substitute
29. Backyard pavilion
30. Mac alternatives: Abbr.
33. Marner of fiction
34. Doesn't allow to gather dust
36. Big name in razors
37. Pique, as one's appetite
38. Body art, briefly

39. "As I see it," in email

40. "Neither fish ___ fowl"

41. Car-cleaning cloth

ANSWERS ON PAGE 254.

CUBIC ZIRCONIA

ACROSS

1. Limber
6. RN treatment
9. Demand, as a price
12. FedEX won't deliver to one
13. Written hugs
14. On the _____ vive (watchful)
15. Vigor
16. Cut of cubic zirconia
18. Cleo's snake
19. Big basin
21. Les _____-Unis (the United States, in France)
22. "_____ the season..."
23. Goof up
24. Cut of cubic zirconia
28. _____ Chen shoes
31. Leave at the altar
32. Winter mo.
33. Pineapple platation island
34. The sun, personified
35. Cut of cubic zirconia
37. Calif. airport: abbr.
39. Peas' place
40. "Watch it wiggle, see it jiggle" dessert
43. Society newcomer
44. Genesis vessel
47. Cut of cubic zirconia

49. Counterindicate
51. En preceders
52. Culpa preceder
53. Like a vacuum
54. Kind of flour or whiskey
55. Cheer of a sort
56. Deceptive ploys

DOWN

1. Grp. for Nancy Lopez
2. Acknowledgements of debt
3. Cook's meas.
4. On everyone's wish list
5. Foreign
6. Pyramid, to a Pharaoh
7. Mauna _____
8. Cider-making device
9. Light greenish blue
10. Executive, slangily
11. Bride's greeting
17. Fiscal time frame: abbr.
20. Having had some experience in
22. "The Closer" network
23. Getaway
24. Slumber party wear, for short
25. Spanish river
26. Not well
27. Consult
28. Glass vessel
29. "I guessed it!"
30. Rustic affirmative

218

33. Quaint
36. Robin Hood, for one
37. Camera type: abbr.
38. Lather-laden
40. Fan's disapproval
41. TV award
42. _____ majesty (act of treason)

43. WWII milestone
44. Swiss peaks
45. Solemn act
46. Custodian's jinglers
48. Actress Thompson
50. Flightless fowl in the outback

ANSWERS ON PAGE 255.

CHARLES MANSON

ACROSS

1. Peter Max genre
7. Preparing for combat
13. Irregular in quality
14. Deli patron's request
15. What Manson called his macabre killing plan, borrowing the 1968 Beatles song
17. Length x width, for a rectangle
18. Auto club inits.
19. Inactive: Abbr.
20. '40s Treasury issue
22. Like boring writing
24. "Shoo!"
25. Baby goat sound
26. Faun-like deity
29. Had regrets
33. 1996 Olympic torch lighter
34. Totally control
35. Brass band boomer
36. Manson, a musician, named his 1970 album "Lie: The ___ Cult"
40. 1912 Olympics star Jim
41. Out jogging
42. Gets smart with
43. Transfers a rootbound begonia, say

DOWN

1. "Fiddlesticks!"
2. "Tosca" or "Carmen"
3. Gondola mover
4. "Way to go, guy!"
5. 1 or 66, e.g.
6. Dictatorial ruler
7. "Crazy Love" singer Paul
8. Beluga eggs
9. 2050, in old Rome
10. Physician: Comb. form
11. Moscow negatives
12. Berry of Motown
16. Feeling blue
21. "___ Town": Wilder
22. Good buddy
23. Dilapidated digs
25. Trusted adviser
26. Epsom and the like
27. Island welcome
28. Records for later viewing, colloquially
29. E-mail directive: Abbr.
30. Grand Canyon pack animal
31. In the area
32. Does some mending
34. Low bills
37. Places to see M.D.'s in a hurry

38. Donkey Kong or King Kong

39. Direction from L.A. to N.Y.

ANSWERS ON PAGE 255.

NCIS

ACROSS

1. Bridgelike game without bidding
6. Very commonplace
11. From that point on
12. "Fingers crossed!"
13. Mark Harmon plays this investigator on NCIS
15. Weather-vane turner
16. Inits. on a battleship
17. Cheese in a Greek salad
20. Crookshanks, in Harry Potter fiction
22. Hollywood legend Gardner
23. Superman accessory
27. Linda Hunt is ___ Lange on NCIS: Los Angeles
29. David McCallum is NCIS Medical Examiner Dr. Donald Mallard, nicknamed ___
30. Pass on the street
32. Carbon-14 determination
33. NY-to-Bermuda dir.
34. Leaky tire sound
35. Reactions to new babies
38. Ultimatum ender, often

40. Kensi Blye on NCIS: Los Angeles is played by ___
45. Emmy or Oscar
46. Planning to, informally
47. Wizards of old
48. Going overboard, for short

DOWN

1. Financial daily, briefly
2. Get a move on, quaintly
3. Savings acct. accrual
4. The "a" sound in "above"
5. "Desperate Housewives" actress Hatcher
6. 1999 Adam Sandler movie
7. Hawaiian tuna
8. De Niro's Manhattan restaurant
9. Alerts from the LAPD
10. "I took the one ___ traveled by": Frost
14. Start of a bedtime story
17. Late Saudi king
18. Till the cows come home
19. Jacques of "Mon Oncle"
21. Sch. of the Horned Frogs

23. Cereal grains in some bread
24. Berry at health food stores
25. UPS deliveries
26. Looks closely at
28. Sports bar screens
31. School starter
34. Salome danced for him
35. Eden evictee

36. Muted trumpet wail
37. Fishing line mishap
39. Starch from a tropical palm
41. Ticked-off feeling
42. Athlete's wear, for short
43. "Barbara ___" (Beach Boys classic)
44. "Macbeth" cauldron stirrer

ANSWERS ON PAGE 255.

MAGICAL WORLD OF TEA

ACROSS

1. Feed for a fee, as cattle
5. Remove with teeth: 2 wds.
11. Moon goddess
12. Abbr. on a map
13. ___ Lingus, Irish carrier
14. Symbol of life
15. Japanese ceremonial beverage: 2 wds.
17. Secret agent's work
19. Genetic fingerprint
20. Scott ___, actor
22. Type of wave
26. Language spoken along the African coast
28. Coal deposit
30. Very long sentence
31. Publisher's employees, for short
32. Indian tea state
34. Mortgage ratio: abbr.
35. Small really badly
37. Vehicle shoe
38. ___ Messi, soccer star
39. Ponzi scheme, e.g
41. Basketball dunk
43. Old PC platform: abbr.
45. Forever, old-style
48. Drink of soaked leaves
52. Origin
53. Padre ___, Italian friar canonized in 2002

54. Suffix with eloqu
55. "Hurry up!"
56. Burn slowly with no flame
57. African howler

DOWN

1. "Too bad"
2. Explosive source of theine
3. Pitch-black
4. Indian title
5. Calc. key
6. Pay attention to
7. Sports, e.g.
8. Cereal ingredient
9. Service charge
10. Italian monk
12. Most custardy
16. Execute perfecly
18. Astronaut's employer
21. Desert retreat
23. Pickle herb
24. Time for the siesta
25. Turning counterclockwise
26. Cut made by a saw
27. Away from port
29. ___ Dietrich, actress
33. Vegan's no-no
36. Spiral-horned cousin of caribou
40. Given medicine
42. Compassion

44. Trig functon
46. Where the Colosseum is
47. European active erupter
48. Internet addresses: abbr.
49. Matchsticks game
50. ___ Fighters, rock band
51. Text-reading tech.

1	2	3	4		■	5	6	7		8	9	10
11				■	12				■	13		
14				■	15			16				
17				18		■	19			■	■	■
■		■	20			21	■	22		23	24	25
26		27	■	28			29	■	30			
31				32				33	■	34		
35			36	■	37				■	38		
39				40		41			42	■		■
■		■	43		44	■	45			46		47
48	49	50			■	51		■	52			
53			■	54				■	55			
56						■	57					

ANSWERS ON PAGE 256.

NEW YEAR'S EVE

ACROSS

1. Mischief
5. Junk bond rating
8. Fashionable
12. Iris holder
13. Kind of dye
14. Rounds
15. Mild epilepsy: 2 wds.
17. Vegetarian protein source
18. Make merry
21. Paper size: abbr.
22. Construct
25. "If you ask me", in texts
28. Big screen theater
31. Physique, informally
32. Beat badly
33. Prince Valiant's son
34. Archangel's headwear
35. High school subj.
36. Foul mood
37. From square one
38. "Whoopee!"
40. On a blood test: abbr.
42. Bubbly drink
47. Pipe problem
50. Vientiane citizens
52. Glacial ridge
53. Aggregation, for short
54. Eyelid sore
55. Fall mo.
56. Tree feller
57. Elaborate fraud

DOWN

1. March sound
2. "Voulez-vous coucher ___ moi, ce soir?"
3. Anatomical nerve network
4. Type of swimsuit
5. From 544 million to about 500 million years ago
6. Industry big shot
7. Caffeine source
8. Provide food for the party
9. Medical care grp.
10. Global lending org.
11. Right before launch
16. Hanoi holiday
19. Cowboy's moniker
20. July 4 show
23. "Voice of Israel" author
24. ___slaw
26. ___ Lisa
27. Grant or Jackman
29. Hosp. scan
30. Rebel church leader
34. Ugly, wrinkled
36. Between fah and lah in Covent Garden
39. Eight musicians
41. Hood's gun
43. Pond dweller
44. Karl or Groucho

226

45. Western defense grp.
46. "May It Be" singer
48. Oil-rich fed.

49. "Without male issue", in Latin: abbr.
51. They say it sells

ANSWERS ON PAGE 256.

ANSWERS

AMERICAN FOLK TALES (PAGE 4)

```
S L A V █ A I D █ █ I S L A
T A R O █ U N O █ S H I P
A M A T █ G R U E S O M E
B A B E T H E B L U E O X
█ █ █ R O T █ L E E █ █ █
R A D I O █ L E V █ D I M
M A I D O F T H E M I S T
N U N █ F E D █ N I K O N
█ █ █ A T A █ I T S █ █ █
J I G G E R J O H N S O N
A L L I N F U N █ A L L Y
P E A L █ U N I █ M A L E
E S M E █ L E A █ E T A T
```

SIDE DISHES (PAGE 8)

```
A L B S █ W A N █ L E G S
S I R E █ E L I █ O L I O
E E O C █ B O T █ F A L L
C U C U M B E R S A L A D
█ █ C R A Y █ A T T █ █
G O O E Y █ A T E █ E R R
O W L S █ A L E █ O X O X
W W I █ A U F █ F R I E S
█ █ O P S █ S H O T █ █
R O A S T P O T A T O E S
A N T I █ I V Y █ U N T O
M I T E █ C E L █ N L R B
S T A R █ E R E █ D Y E S
```

WHAT'S COOKING (PAGE 6)

```
T E C H █ T A B █ G A T E
A R M Y █ V C R █ E N V Y
U N S E T T L E █ N O M E
█ █ N I A █ V O X █ █
S C R A M B L E D E G G S
L A H █ E L O █ E R R O L
I R I S █ E T C █ S E R A
T E N P M █ T U B █ C S T
S W E E T P O T A T O E S
█ █ E V E █ O B I █ █
V O I D █ C O P Y B O O K
I S L E █ A R E █ I N R E
S E A R █ N O N █ A S E A
```

ONE OF THE STAR WARS (PAGE 10)

```
█ O B I W A N K E N O B I
C █ L █ A █ A █ L █ P █ N
A M A █ T I G H T S H I P
T █ S █ C █ █ O █ E █ U
N O T C H █ S A N D L O T
A █ █ I █ O █ █ I █ █
P H A N T O M M E N A C E
█ N █ █ M █ N █ █ █ L
A T T A C H E █ D E B R A
P █ E █ H █ █ G █ R █ P
P E N S A C O L A █ A D S
L █ N █ S █ R █ M █ V █ E
E W A N M C G R E G O R █
```

ANSWERS

IT'S ALL IN HOW YOU READ IT (PAGE 12)

```
L E A H   D O A   G O B S
A R L O   U R N   E L A H
W I I G   M E A   N E N E
N E I G H B O R H O O D
      I B O   C I A
T O R S O   V H S   F A T
U H O H   D I Y   B O S H
T M I   P E A   A R O S E
      A I M   E R A
  S U B C O N S C I O U S
F A S O   T O T   D E R M
A G E D   E T E   E N D O
B A S E   D E E   D O U G
```

SEE CRUISE (PAGE 16)

```
  J E R R Y M A G U I R E
P   A   A   E   E   M   V
A U G   I L L A T E A S E
S   E   L     B   G   N
T H R O W   P A Y D I R T
O     A   L       N
R I S K Y B U S I N E S S
    T   M   N       C
D R E S S U P   F I B E R
A   P   I     A   A   I
F R O M N O W O N   Y A P
O   N   E   E   T   O   T
E Y E S W I D E S H U T
```

MERYL STREEP MOVIES (PAGE 14)

```
M O C S   M A D   M P A A
S P A T   I P A   A R M S
N A B E   S O I T G O E S
  H O P E S P R I N G S
      S T Y   Y S E R
B A D   T O M   T A P A
T H E L A U N D R O M A T
W I F E   O R E   S T E
    A A A A   A N T
  S U F F R A G E T T E
W E L L T O D O   O N U S
E R T E   A U F   P U R E
E A S T   R E F   S T O W
```

COMFY AT HOME (PAGE 18)

```
W A R D   P O P   H A F T
A C A I   I P A   I R I S
A T M S   X E R   G I N A
C A P T A I N S C H A I R
      U K E   L A C
W H E R E   L E S   C D S
P O T B E L L Y S T O V E
M I C   L I D   I O N I A
      J A B   E N O
F E A T H E R P I L L O W
R E F I   R E C   B A S H
E L A L   A N O   O I S E
E Y R E   L O T   X R A Y
```

ARTHURIAN LEGEND (PAGE 20)

E	C	H	O		A	R	T	H	U	R
L	O	O	N		C	E	R	I	S	E
B	I	L	E		R	I	O	T	E	D
A	N	Y		T	I	N	Y			
		G	E	O	D	E		E	R	A
S	C	R	I	M		D	I	X	O	N
W	E	A	R			O	C	A	S	
A	R	I	E	S		S	W	A	M	I
P	A	L		T	O	T	A	L		
		B	I	N	D		I	L	K	
A	S	S	E	T	S		A	B	E	R
S	O	U	R	C	E		S	U	F	I
K	N	I	G	H	T		A	R	T	S

DIRECTED BY CLINT EASTWOOD (PAGE 24)

P	A	L	E		S	R	S		S	P	A	T
I	R	O	C		O	O	H		E	R	I	E
U	M	B	R	E	L	L	A		M	E	R	E
		U	N	F	O	R	G	I	V	E	N	
N	A	U	S	E	A		P	A	P	I		
E	M	S			M	I	S	R	E	A	D	
A	B	S	O	L	U	T	E	P	O	W	E	R
P	I	E	P	A	N	S			E	R	A	
	N	E	I	N		R	A	N	D	O	M	
G	R	A	N	T	O	R	I	N	O			
L	O	T	S		T	E	A	T	O	W	E	L
O	B	O	E		E	N	T		B	I	R	D
B	E	R	T		D	E	A		S	I	R	S

FIND THE CITY (PAGE 22)

GOING TOW TO TOE (PAGE 26)

ANSWERS

ROCKET MAN (PAGE 28)

```
T O M W O L F E . A C E S
H . I . F . B . . H . H
R V S . U N I T P R I C E
O . S . S . . U . N . R
W R I T E I N . M I A M I
. . L . . O . P . . F
T H E R I G H T S T U F F
H . . D . O . . P
A T B A T . W A S H T U B
T . R . A . . E . O . O
S W I N G V O T E . P I N
I . D . . D . Y . A . U
T E E N . E D H A R R I S
```

FOWL LANGUAGE (PAGE 32)

```
. G O B B L E D E G O O K
. N . E . L . S . F . E
T R Y M E . F I S H F R Y
A . O . S . . E . D . P
S Q U A W K B O X . U S A
K . A . R . . T . D
. F O X W O R T H Y
W . I . . O . A . . S
E R S . D U M B C L U C K
A . H . W . . K . N . I
S U N D E C K . S O C K S
E . E . L . G . U . L
L I T T L E B O P E E P
```

MOVIE REMAKES (PAGE 30)

```
F A M E . P B S . P G D N
I B I S . L O T . E U R O
T E N T S A L E . D A U B
. T H E L I O N K I N G
. . S Y D . C O C A
F A R . . H I B A C H I
T H E J U N G L E B O O K
D I S A V O W . . S E E
. I M E D . M R T
. A S T A R I S B O R N
A L T A . A D D I T I O N
D O O R . M O O . A G U E
C E R T . A L S . L A N D
```

CHARACTERS WE LOVE (PAGE 34)

```
S P E C . O W L S . H I D
T A C O . U H O H . E D U
U P O N . T I V O . R E T
N A N C Y D R E W . M A Y
. . L O O . D E M I
C A J U N . T I R E O U T
B R A D . S I T . A N T S
S E N E G A L . S N E A K
. E D A M . D O W
O B E . R O B I N H O O D
P A Y . A V E R . I D L E
E R R . G A N G . L O I N
N E E . E R T E . E R O S
```

ANSWERS

THE HALF-MARATHON (PAGE 36)

I	M	G	O	O	D	A	T	T	H	E	
N		H		P		B		A		B	S
S	P	A	R	E	M	E		P	A	B	L	O
O		N		N		D		T		N	
	C	A	R	B	O	L	O	A	D	I	N	G
		A		E		N		D			
I	N	F	E	R	N	O		C	L	E	A	N
M		A		N		E					E
B	U	T	I	S	K	I	P		A	S	I	S
I		C		L		G		C		T
B	R	A	V	O		T	W	O	T	I	M	E
E		T		T		A		W		F	G
		T	H	E	R	U	N	N	I	N	G

WILD ANIMALS (PAGE 40)

G	E	N	T	L	E	A	S	A	B	A	L	M
O		O		O		T		D		R		O
U	P	S	E	T		A	T	E	D	I	R	T
D		W		S		L		P		Z		L
A	G	E	S	A	G	O		T	B	O	N	E
		A				S				N		Y
G	E	T	O	N	E	S	T	O	G	A	
U			E				N					W
L	A	L	A	W		A	T	L	A	R	G	E
C		U		B		Z		E		U		N
H	A	N	D	O	U	T		A	T	B	A	T
E		A		R		E		V		I		I
S	P	R	I	N	G	C	H	E	C	K	I	N

HELLO, AUSSIES (PAGE 38)

T	A	K	E			E	M	S	P	A	C	E
I	D	O	L		P	L	A	T	Y	P	U	S
B	L	A	U		O	R	N	A	M	E	N	T
B	I	L	L	A	B	O	N	G		M	E	R
S	B	A		O	O	P	S		A	A	A
		C	R	Y	O		T	E	S	T	Y
	O	D	E	T	S		S	H	A	K	E
K	U	A	L	A		W	H	I	R	
A	T	V		F	O	I	E		E	M	T
R	B	I		D	O	W	N	U	N	D	E	R
M	A	N	P	U	R	S	E		U	S	D	A
A	C	C	E	N	T	E	D		T	E	E	M
S	K	I	N	N	E	R		S	L	A	P

IN THE LONG RUN (PAGE 42)

A	B	C	D		M	A	R	A	T	H	O	N
F	I	L	I	A	L		U	L	U			
T	O	A	D		B	O	D	Y	T	Y	P	E
E	M	S		O		W	E	N		I	A	N
R	E	P	O	R	T	E	R		R	E	T	D
			C	L	A	D		H	E	L	I	O
B	O	S	T	O	N		L	O	N	D	O	N
I	N	C	A	N		L	I	M	A	
G	A	U	L		F	U	T	I	L	I	T	Y
H	I	T		B	O	X		E		N	H	A
T	R	A	W	L	N	E	T		B	L	E	W
			A	U	D		H	A	R	A	R	E
F	O	O	T	R	A	C	E		A	W	E	D

ANSWERS

GETTING ARTY (PAGE 44)

S	L	A	P		V	M	I		N	O	T	E
L	A	Z	E		E	A	R		A	D	A	M
A	D	I	N		T	H	A	W	S	O	U	T
B	Y	Z	A	N	T	I	N	E	A	R	T	
		N	E	E		I	L	L				
A	M	O	C	O		P	A	L		A	A	U
C	A	V	E	P	A	I	N	T	I	N	G	S
E	R	A		H	I	T		O	N	I	O	N
		O	Y	L		O	D	D				
	C	O	N	T	E	M	P	O	R	A	R	Y
F	O	R	T	E	R	I	E		I	R	I	S
L	I	Z	A		O	A	R		V	I	S	E
A	T	O	P		N	S	A		E	D	E	R

HORSE OPERAS (PAGE 48)

A	D	E	N		P	I	E		P	L	A	N
T	I	P	I		A	D	M		L	A	C	Y
A	S	E	A		W	E	E		I	N	R	E
T	H	E	L	O	N	E	R	A	N	G	E	R
		O	W	S		I	L	K				
G	W	Y	N	N		A	T	L		I	C	U
T	H	E	G	U	N	F	I	G	H	T	E	R
O	O	P		P	E	T		O	A	T	E	N
		I	T	O		C	N	N				
F	A	S	T	O	N	T	H	E	D	R	A	W
A	B	I	G		O	I	L		B	U	O	Y
H	U	T	U		I	D	O		A	N	N	S
D	D	A	Y		R	Y	E		G	E	E	S

CLOTHES AND ACCESSORIES (PAGE 46)

	C	N	N		M	P	S		S	C	A	D
U	P	T	O		E	L	S		O	R	Z	O
	S	H	E	T	L	A	N	D	W	O	O	L
S		L	I	E	N			W	T	O		
W	B	C		P	E	A	T		B	E	E	R
A	L	I	S	T		R	I	C	O			
B	U	T	T	O	N		M	O	H	A	I	R
	A	P	O	C		H	O	R	S	E		
P	O	L	Y		S	O	H	O		C	O	N
S	K	I		B	U	S	S				D	
H	A	B	E	R	D	A	S	H	E	R	Y	
A	P	E	X		B	I	S		A	O	R	B
W	I	L	T		A	N	Y		N	W	S	

PARASITE (PAGE 50)

F	L	Y		B	O	N	G		D	I	S	H
L	O	A		E	L	A	L		E	M	I	R
A	P	P		A	E	R	O		E	P	P	S
B	E	S	T	P	I	C	T	U	R	E		
		W	A	C		T	H	E	R	O	D	
D	E	V	I	L		G	I	S		I	O	I
O	V	E	N		I	N	S		G	A	Z	E
F	A	R		E	T	C		A	R	L	E	S
F	L	Y	E	R	S		T	V	A			
	F	E	A	T	U	R	E	F	I	L	M	
F	A	I	R		R	V	E	R		P	A	Y
M	U	N	I		U	E	Y	S		A	N	T
S	K	E	E		E	A	S	E		D	A	H

ANSWERS

GRANDMA'S PANTRY (PAGE 52)

BADDIES OF FICTION (PAGE 56)

FINISH THE ADAGE (PAGE 54)

SORRY (PAGE 58)

DRIVING AROUND (PAGE 60)

```
S A S S I N G   L E A P T
I D I D T O O   U L T R A
D I C I E S T   X Y L E M
E E E     T A B U   A T T
B U M P E R C A R   N E A
    U S A   S Y S T E M
F L I R T       C Y A N S
L I N E A L   P A N
A V A   T E N O R C L E F
T E T   E D I T     A R E
B O R I C   P A R T I A L
E N O L A   A G A I N S T
D E T E R   T E E P E E S
```

OLD PRINTING HOUSE (PAGE 64)

```
T R A P   P R E   A G R A
S A R I   L E D   I R I S
K P M G   A N I   K I N K
  T Y P E S E T T I N G
P   E L M W O O D       P
R U A N D A   R O O F E R
E S P             L E I
S A T A N G   I N T U R N
S   T H R O M B I       T
  R O L L O F P A P E R
R I G A   U T E   T G I F
I D E S   S E N   O G L E
M E E T   E N D   E Y E D
```

DAVID O. RUSSELL MOVIES (PAGE 62)

```
P S A L M   A L F I E
F E M U R   P E E R S
F T O R D   B A N A L
T H R E E K I N G S
      D E M O N S
L I P I D S   H M M
E A R N S   B O U G H
O N E   D E N I R O
    C R A V A T
  T H E F I G H T E R
J O I S T   L E A V E
O G L E R   E D D A S
Y A L T A   S L A N T
```

YOU WANNA PIECE O' ME? (PAGE 66)

```
  L O S E Y O U R H E A D
S   R   R   F   A   A   E
C H I N A   F L Y T R A P
U   O   K       N   O
L E N D A N E A R   E A T
P   X   Y   H   S
T E C H I E   B O T T O M
    R   N   E   D       A
G U Y   G I V E A H A N D
I   W       E       L   E
Z O O M S I N   F E T I D
M   L   I   S   D   A   O
O F F E R Y O U R A R M
```

ANSWERS

TO KILL A MOCKINGBIRD (PAGE 68)

PHILHARMONIC (PAGE 72)

YOGA CLASS (PAGE 70)

FICTIONAL PLACES (PAGE 74)

ANSWERS

GODS OF THE OCEANS
(PAGE 76)

MEDICAL RESEARCH
(PAGE 80)

ONCE UPON A TIME...IN HOLLYWOOD (PAGE 78)

13-LETTER WORDS
(PAGE 82)

ANSWERS

OLD VIDEO GAMES (PAGE 84)

BLUE BLOODS (PAGE 88)

BUILDING SITE (PAGE 86)

SCARY MONSTERS (PAGE 90)

238

GAS STATION (PAGE 92)

P	H	S			S	L	A		A	S	S
H	A	T	E		D	E	A	R		L	A	H
A	J	A	X		O	R	S	O		A	G	E
T	I	R	E	P	R	E	S	S	U	R	E	
		C	I	S		O	E	R				
B	B	C		M	E	W			A	S	A	P
R	A	D	I	A	T	O	R	F	L	U	I	D
B	A	S	S		W	E	I		E	L	F	
		N	O	D		M	S	C				
	M	O	T	O	R	V	E	H	I	C	L	E
G	O	B		H	I	E	D		T	A	E	L
D	U	O		E	E	R	Y		Y	L	E	M
P	E	E		D	D	T			F	R	Y	

IN THE DOJO (PAGE 96)

O	C	A		M	A	D	E		S	P	E	W
M	S	N		A	P	I	A		E	L	M	S
B	A	C	K	F	I	S	T		N	S	F	W
			A	I	S		S	A	S			
S	A	U	N	A		M		R	E	A	C	T
H	I	N	T		M	A	N	T	I	L	L	A
A	D	D		L	I	V	R	E		T	O	M
L	E	U	K	E	M	I	A		S	H	A	M
T	R	E	A	T		S		K	O	O	K	Y
			R	O	E		A	N	U			
A	G	F	A		S	I	D	E	K	I	C	K
O	M	I	T		O	P	E	L		R	H	O
K	O	B	E		P	O	S	T		K	I	D

GONE FISHIN' (PAGE 94)

S	A	L	M	O	N		W	H	A	L	E	S
T	R	Y	O	N	E		B	Y	R	O	T	E
O	T	E	L	L	O		C	A	T	B	O	X
W	E	S	T	E	N	D		T	D	S		
			S	A	A	B		T	E	T	R	A
E	E	L		S	T	A	R		C	E	O	S
A	Z	A	L	E	A		A	C	O	R	N	S
T	I	R	E		L	A	V	A		S	A	T
S	O	G	G	Y		S	I	R	S			
		E	A	U		P	O	W	E	R	P	C
C	A	S	T	R	O		L	A	G	U	N	A
O	N	S	E	T	S		I	S	A	D	O	R
D	O	E	S	S	O		S	H	R	I	M	P

BEAUTY OF CHESS (PAGE 98)

T	O	M	B		S	I	C	I	L	I	A	N
A	B	B	R		O	T	O			A	D	A
B	E	A	U		I	L	L	T	I	M	E	D
			C	A	L	L	O	U	S			
B	A	L	E	D				B	A	S	I	L
I	G	A		D	U	C	T		A	C	C	A
R	O	B	E	R	T	F	I	S	C	H	E	R
C	R	O	C		C	L	U	E		M	U	G
H	A	R	A	M			M	Y	O	P	E
			S	O	M	A	L	I	A			
H	I	G	H	W	I	R	E		M	A	T	T
A	B	U		N	G	O		E	B	B	S	
N	O	T	A	T	I	O	N		N	Y	S	E

VERY COLD (PAGE 100)

```
D O J O   F R E E Z I N G
E X A M   L A W   A V I A
G O R E   O V E R C A L L O
R     N A P E R Y       O
E E C   A     A P B   O
E T H E R E A L   O A S T
  T E M P E R A T U R E
B A L I   G A S I F I E D
A   A T V     N   C P R
R     A L W A Y S     Y
B R A I N I A C   A L I I
R U N T   E T H   N A R C
A B S O L U T E   E R S E
```

SWARM OF HONEYMAKERS (PAGE 104)

```
S A T I R I Z E   S T O P
C F O   E R I N   T O R R
U R L   H O P E   A R C O
P O L L E N   M O B C A P
    C A M   A L L     O
Q U A D R A T   D E V I L
U V C   N A B     P O I
E A T O N   T E T A N U S
E   C F C   R E B
N O D U L E   N E C T A R
B O I L   A M A H   Z O O
E Z R A   S O R E   A N A
E Y E R   E N D E A R E D
```

MARVEL-OUS MOVIES (PAGE 102)

```
T H O R   D E F   H U L K
R E N O   E T E   O N E A
A R K S   N O R   E A V E
C A P T A I N M A R V E L
    R P M   E N S O R
S E T U P   E N D   W A S
M A A M   R E T   L E G O
U R I   A Y E   C A D E T
  B L I N K   I C Y
D O C T O R S T R A N G E
O N O S   I T S   B A R D
S E A M   S A O   E N I D
E S T E   P R N   T A D A
```

ARCHEOLOGY (PAGE 106)

```
A C C T   A L P S   W A G
S H I A   S E A T   E C U
C U R B   P Y R A M I D S
I N C U B I   D I O R
I K E   O R A   R A D A R
    B W A N A   T I L T
A N C I E N T G R E E C E
G O O K   T R I A D
T H A I S   A T I   D P I
    S N O W   A D J O I N
A R T I F A C T   A L L A
M E A   A G I O   K E E P
S M L   R E A R   E D I T
```

ANSWERS

PAINTINGS (PAGE 108)

GRETA GERWIG (PAGE 112)

WINTER FLYING SPORT (PAGE 110)

STAY HEALTHY (PAGE 114)

ANSWERS

TERMINATOR-LIKE FUTURE (PAGE 116)

NAVAL WARFARE (PAGE 120)

THAT'S A NO-NO (PAGE 118)

IN THE OPERA (PAGE 122)

ANSWERS

VOLCANIC ACTIVITY
(PAGE 124)

GETTING MARRIED
(PAGE 128)

SAOIRSE RONAN MOVIES
(PAGE 126)

ECOLOGY (PAGE 130)

ANSWERS

DENTAL HEALTH
(PAGE 132)

U	R	G	E	R		T	E	N		H	I	S
V	E	R	D	I		A	D	E	N	I	N	E
B	E	A	D	Y		C	H	E	C	K	U	P
		N	O	A	H			D	O	E	S	T
A	S	T		D	Y	L	A	N		R	E	A
T	O	O	T	H	P	A	S	T	E			
T	O	R	I		H	R	S		C	R	A	N
		P	R	E	V	E	N	T	I	O	N	
W	F	H		E	N	A	T	E		N	L	E
E	L	A	N	D			S	T	A	G		
N	O	S	U	G	A	R		T	U	L	S	A
C	O	N	T	U	S	E		L	E	E	R	Y
H	R	T		M	A	T		E	L	T	O	N

IN THE VINEYARD
(PAGE 136)

C	R	A	W		F	L	A	K		T	Z	E
H	E	R	E		L	I	N	E		E	E	L
A	G	U	A		O	A	K	Y		N	E	O
T	A	B	L	E	G	R	A	P	E	S		
E	L	A	T	E				A	T	E	I	N
A			H	E	R	A	L	D	I	S	T	
U	P	C			A	M	T			T	A	W
	S	O	T	O	S	P	E	A	K			I
S	T	R	U	T				T	I	T	A	N
	V	I	T	I	C	U	L	T	U	R	E	
S	R	I		A	M	E	R		B	L	O	B
I	O	N		W	A	N	E		A	L	M	A
S	A	E		A	N	T	A		G	E	A	R

__ HO! (PAGE 134)

I	O	W	A		O	L	D		L	A	S	H
T	T	O	P		V	I	I		A	R	I	A
C	R	O	P	L	A	N	D		W	E	A	N
H	O	L	L	Y		E	N	G	L	A	N	D
			Y	O	U		T	O	E			
D	A	Y		N	A	B		O	S	I	E	R
E	D	A	M		R	I	D		S	O	M	E
C	O	P	R	A		N	O	D		N	U	T
			C	D	S		N	E	T			
G	A	R	L	A	N	D		S	I	C	K	O
E	R	I	E		A	U	C	K	L	A	N	D
E	T	T	A		C	P	O		E	G	A	D
K	E	E	N		K	E	G		X	E	R	S

ITALIAN FOOD (PAGE 138)

R	A	V	E	R		P	M	S		P	G	A
O	P	I	N	E		U	K	E		E	R	N
S	P	A	G	H	E	T	T	I		C	I	D
A	T	L	E	A	S	T		Z	L	O	T	Y
			L	B	S		B	I	E	R		
C	O	P	S			N	A	N	K	I	N	G
H	U	A		D	O	I	N	G		N	A	M
G	I	R	L	I	S	H			S	O	Y	A
		M	A	S	S		H	E	T			
D	O	E	T	H		S	E	V	E	R	A	L
A	W	S		P	E	P	P	E	R	O	N	I
D	E	A		A	M	A		R	E	C	C	E
A	N	N		N	U	N		Y	O	K	E	D

HIGH IN THE MOUNTAINS (PAGE 140)

A	A	A	S		C	O	S		W	A	R	D
T	A	L	C		O	P	P		E	R	I	E
M	A	K	O		H	E	A	D	L	A	M	P
		A	U	T	O			I	S	L	E	T
Y	A	L	T	A		S	A	S	H			
A	P	I		B	R	I	L	L		O	D	A
W	A	F	F	L	E	S	T	O	M	P	E	R
P	R	Y		E	S	S	A	Y		E	M	I
		A	T	T	Y		A	N	N	I	E	
A	U	D	I	O			A	L	E	S		
C	R	A	M	P	O	N	S		G	H	A	T
T	I	M	E		N	A	H		R	O	V	E
A	C	E	R		T	V	Y		O	P	E	D

BARREN AND LIFELESS (PAGE 144)

S	I	R		S	P	I	L	L		A	R	P
E	P	I		T	O	D	O	S		C	A	L
W	A	S	T	E	L	A	N	D		E	V	A
A		O	H	I	O		E		F	R	E	T
R	A	T	O	N		E	N	N	O	B	L	E
D	I	T		C	R	E	E	L				
	G	O	D	F	O	R	S	A	K	E	N	
		A	I	R	E	S			M	A	S	
P	R	E	T	E	N	D		T	R	E	N	T
Y	O	R	E		B		A	V	E	R		E
X	O	O		D	E	A	D	S	W	A	M	P
I	T	S		A	L	G	A	E		L	O	U
E	Y	E		S	T	A	R	T		D	I	P

MEDIEVAL CAVALRY CLASH (PAGE 142)

R	B	I		B	A	J	A		T	H	U	G
F	W	D		A	C	E	D		H	O	P	I
D	I	S	A	B	L	E	D		Y	V	E	S
		T	O	U	R	N	A	M	E	N	T	
H	A	L	L	O			B	Y	R	D		
A	S	I	A		P	L	E	B				C
J	O	U	S	T	I	N	G	A	R	E	N	A
J			Y	E	G	G		E	M	A	G	
	P	E	A	K			S	T	O	G	Y	
P	L	A	T	E	A	R	M	O	R			
S	A	G	O		L	O	O	N	Y	B	I	N
S	T	E	M		B	L	I	N		B	B	L
T	O	R	Y		A	L	L	Y		B	M	W

MISHMASH (PAGE 146)

S	K	I	R	M	I	S	H		C	H	O	W
Y		N		A		C		H		A		I
R	U	S	T	L	E	R		E	V	I	C	T
U		P		T		U		A		T		N
P	I	E	C	E	O	F	A	D	V	I	C	E
	C		S		F		S				S	
G	A	T	H	E	R		J	O	K	E	R	S
O			C			G		F		N		
T	H	E	F	R	I	A	R	S	C	L	U	B
A		L		O		U		T		A		O
J	E	D	I	S		C	H	A	G	R	I	N
O		E		S		H		T		G		U
B	A	R	B		M	O	D	E	L	E	R	S

ANSWERS

PC HARDWARE (PAGE 148)

B	A	H		A	B	E	D		B	L	I	P
O	N	E		V	I	V	A		L	I	C	E
A	T	E		O	V	E	N		U	S	E	R
S	I	L	I	C	O	N	C	H	I	P		S
		L	E	U		E	O	N				O
C	O	A	L	T	A	R		E	G	G	O	N
O	D	D		C	A	P			E	R	A	
M	E	O	W	S		G	E	N	T	E	E	L
P		H	A	P		T	O	W				
U	M	O	T	H	E	R	B	O	A	R	D	
T	E	A	L		I	D	O	L		B	A	Y
E	V	I	L		A	G	U	E		L	I	E
R	E	L	Y		L	E	S	S		E	N	S

POP STARS (PAGE 152)

F	I	B	S		B	I	T		S	T	L	O
O	K	L	A		A	D	O		T	R	A	P
R	E	V	I	E	W	E	R		A	U	N	T
D	A	D	D	Y	L	O	N	G	L	E	G	S
		H	E	S		A	O	K				
R	E	L	I	C		I	D	I		H	O	B
I	C	E		A	P	R	O	N		A	A	U
G	O	O		N	R	A		D	A	I	R	Y
		I	D	O		A	E	C				
D	A	D	D	Y	W	A	R	B	U	C	K	S
A	C	A	I		L	E	F	T	T	U	R	N
I	M	H	O		E	R	E		E	R	I	A
N	E	S	T		R	O	D		R	E	S	P

MATT DAMON MOVIES (PAGE 150)

A	H	O	Y		E	L	M		A	S	H	E
C	O	M	O		R	O	O		B	O	O	M
T	R	I	D	E	N	T	S		O	L	E	O
I	N	T	E	R	S	T	E	L	L	A	R	
		L	A	T		L	A	I	R			
J	O	B			E	L	Y	S	I	U	M	
A	L	A	S		D	O	E		H	U	M	P
M	A	R	T	I	A	N			M	A	G	
		E	E	N	Y		L	A	G			
	T	H	E	G	R	E	A	T	W	A	L	L
C	H	A	P		A	P	P	L	E	P	I	E
D	A	N	L		T	E	E		N	I	L	E
S	I	D	E		E	E	L		N	A	T	S

LOOK ON THE BRIGHT SIDE (PAGE 154)

W	H	E	W		T	E	A		S	L	I	P
O	A	T	H		I	S	M		R	U	S	E
E	R	N	O		L	A	O		O	S	L	O
S	P	A	R	K	L	I	N	G		T	E	N
		L	E	N		G	N	A	R			
T	A	D		N	O	T		U	S	O	F	A
S	H	A	M		W	W	W		S	U	I	T
K	A	Z	O	O		O	A	K		S	E	E
		Z	E	R	O		L	I	V			
P	O	L		B	R	I	L	L	I	A	N	T
E	M	I	L		A	P	E		V	O	U	S
K	A	N	E		T	O	Y		I	N	K	A
E	R	G	O		E	S	E		D	E	E	R

ANSWERS

IT'S IN YOUR HANDS (PAGE 156)

F	O	O	D		C	H	O	C		T	A	P
I	D	L	E		L	E	A	H		E	T	E
T	I	L	L		A	P	S	O		E	R	N
A	N	A	L	Y	S	T		P	A	N	I	C
S	G	S		O	P	A		S	C	I	F	I
		H	U	E	D		T	C	E	L	L	
P	I	C	A	R	D		M	I	T	R	E	S
A	H	A	L	F		H	I	C	S			
P	A	R	E	U		A	L	K		G	D	S
E	V	E	N	T		M	E	S	S	I	A	H
E	E	E		U	S	M	A		U	T	N	E
T	I	R		R	O	E	G		E	M	I	L
E	T	S		E	I	R	E		T	O	O	L

MISNOMERS (PAGE 160)

H	A	D	J		F	D	R		A	R	I	A
I	D	E	A		R	I	O		S	O	D	A
P	A	R	K	W	A	Y	S		S	E	A	U
	O	W	N		S	E	A					
A	R	A	B	I	C	F	I	G	U	R	E	S
F	E	D		I	I	I		G	L	O	B	E
L	A	M	P		S	E	T		T	U	B	E
A	T	A	R	I		R	U	B		E	E	K
C	A	N	A	R	Y	I	S	L	A	N	D	S
	E	R	A		C	O	O					
A	D	I	T		B	L	A	C	K	B	O	X
T	O	D	O		B	O	N		A	A	R	E
T	H	O	R		A	N	Y		Y	A	R	D

GUESS THE THEME (PAGE 158)

B	E	E	P		S	O	N		T	Y	R	O
U	T	E	S		C	P	U		H	O	O	P
M	A	R	Y		O	A	R		R	Y	A	S
	L	O	C	K	T	H	E	D	O	O	R	
	H	O	T		Y	E	W					
P	A	T	I	O		G	E	L		H	E	R
S	T	O	C	K	D	I	V	I	D	E	N	D
I	M	P		I	O	N		V	O	T	E	S
	E	E	L		T	E	N					
	B	A	R	R	E	L	O	R	G	A	N	
P	U	M	A		O	A	K		L	O	O	T
E	R	O	S		U	S	A		E	N	D	S
T	Y	K	E		T	H	Y		S	E	E	P

FUN FADS (PAGE 162)

I	T	S		C	O	B	S		A	D	E	S
H	U	L	A	H	O	O	P		L	E	V	I
O	N	A	S	L	O	P	E		E	B	A	N
P	A	T	I	O		P	E	T	R	O	C	K
	A	E	C		D	I	O	N				
H	O	G	G		A	I	D	S		A	I	L
T	A	R	O		M	O	I		J	I	B	E
S	K	A		A	P	I	A		A	R	M	S
	V	E	R	B		L	A	W				
C	H	I	A	P	E	T		T	O	G	A	S
N	O	T	V		L	O	O	P	H	O	L	E
B	R	A	E		L	A	V	A	L	A	M	P
C	A	S	S		S	T	A	R		L	S	T

ANSWERS

THE NEXT BIG THING
(PAGE 164)

```
M A S S I V E . H A S T A
I M P E R I L . U B O A T
S A L I E R I . M C D L T
E T A S . T O D O . A L A
R I T . G U T E N . L I I
. . D I E . N G U Y E N
A S P E N . . O P E D S
B A L B O A . D U C .
O V A . R A M U S . S S E
L A N . M A A M . M O O R
I N T R O . O D W A L L A
S N A F U . R U I N O U S
H A R K S . I M M E N S E
```

ADVERTISING MASCOTS
(PAGE 168)

```
N E T . F A R . G L A S S
E D A M A M E . O A T E S
R E T I R E D . O S A G E
F R I T O B A N D I T O
. . T E A N E C K
D Y N E . S T A R . D A D
J O H N F . Y O U R S
S N L . U S S R . N O E L
. G L U C O S E
C H E F B O Y A R D E E
O M A N I . F A T U I T Y
A V R I L . F L A N K E R
F I D E L . S S N . E S E
```

HOLDING HANDS
(PAGE 166)

```
C O M P . W E T . H U G E
O P A L . I R S . A X I S
Y E T I . L I E . R O T E
. C H A N D E L I E R S
. B E E . I S M
P O U L T . K O S . M A Y
T A M E . L I T . C O R E
A R P . R E X . W H I C H
. F A B . A W E .
. W A S H A N D W E A R
T I N T . R E D . S L A P
A L T O . O R E . E E R O
P E E P . N O D . S E E P
```

EVEN AS WE SPOCK
(PAGE 170)

```
. I N S E A R C H O F
. S K . S . H . N
A T E D I R T . A W A K E
A L . E . T U T . I . L
S T Y X . S T A R T R E K
O . O . M . E . O . S
. U T A H . B O W L
C . I . I . M . I . R
L I V E L O N G . A Q U A
A . I . D . D . W . U . M
M I X E R . I G I V E U P
. E . O . G . S . U
A N D P R O S P E R
```

ANSWERS

THE AMERICANS (PAGE 172)

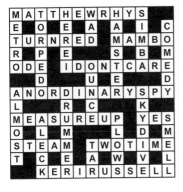

MAHERSHALA ALI MOVIES (PAGE 176)

HIDDEN CLUE (PAGE 174)

GOOD-BYE, GOOD BUY (PAGE 178)

JOHN GOTTI (PAGE 180)

G	A	T	E		D	A	P	P	E	R
A	X	E	L		H	E	A	R	Y	E
R	E	F	I		A	R	G	U	E	D
Y	S	L		O	B	I	E			
			O	L	D	I	E		R	E	B
S	Y	N	O	D		S	T	A	L	E
C	O	D	A			A	C	M	E	
A	L	O	N	G		N	I	K	O	N
M	O	N		A	P	P	L	E		
		S	L	U	R		T	E	E	
M	E	N	T	O	R		M	E	A	L
O	S	C	A	R	S		L	E	S	S
B	O	O	T	E	E		B	R	E	A

HOME AT LAST (PAGE 184)

S	O	M	E		T	R	A	D	E
O	N	A	T		A	I	L	E	D
W	R	I	T	I	N	G	P	A	D
E	A	S	E	R		H	O	L	Y
T	M	I		M	A	T			
O	P	E	R	A	H	O	U	S	E
			U	S	O		N	E	V
S	T	A	S		M	A	I	N	E
T	A	X	S	H	E	L	T	E	R
A	D	I	E	U		S	E	C	T
T	A	S	T	E		O	D	A	S

HOW TO TAKE CHARGE (PAGE 182)

W	A	N	D	A		I	C	I	C	L	E
A	C	E	I	T		C	A	L	L	O	N
R	U	L	E	T	H	E	R	O	O	S	T
M	E	S	S	H	A	L	L		T	E	E
		E	A	T		W	H	I	R		
C	A	L	L	T	H	E	S	H	O	T	S
O	D	A	S		L	O	O				
N	O	L		D	E	A	R	S	I	R	S
C	R	A	C	K	T	H	E	W	H	I	P
H	E	L	E	N	A		S	H	I	V	A
S	E	A	L	Y	S		T	O	T	E	M

GETTING GOOSEBUMPS (PAGE 186)

C	A	T		T	R	I	V	I	A
O	L	E		A	E	N	E	A	S
G	O	E	A	T	W	O	R	M	S
S	E	N	D		N	O	B	U	
			D	N	A		N	I	C
G	H	O	S	T	B	E	A	C	H
R	U	N		H	E	R			
A	M	E	R		I	D	L	E	
B	A	D	H	A	R	E	D	A	Y
A	N	G	E	L	A		A	C	E
T	E	E	O	F	F		Y	E	S

ANSWERS

FUNKY FASHION (PAGE 188)

P	A	C	T		C	A	M	P	S
A	M	O	S		S	C	A	L	A
P	O	R	K	P	I	E	H	A	T
A	R	E	T	E		S	A	N	I
		S	P	A		L	E	N	
K	I	N	K	Y	B	O	O	T	S
A	N	E		S	O	D			
N	F	L	D		D	E	A	N	S
S	A	L	O	P	E	T	T	E	S
A	N	I	M	E		T	O	R	T
S	T	E	E	P		A	P	O	S

FAIR SHARES? (PAGE 192)

P	R	E	S	S			S	H	A
A	I	R	S	E	A		C	I	R
B	E	T	T	E	R	H	A	L	F
A	L	E	S		C	A	L	L	A
				E	A	S	I	E	R
S	E	C	O	N	D	H	A	L	F
T	R	E	N	D	Y				
E	R	L	E	S		C	A	N	E
F	O	L	D	I	N	H	A	L	F
F	R	A		T	H	E	A	R	T
I	S	R		A	R	A	B	S	

FAVE FLAVES (PAGE 190)

W	A	S	H		R	A	T	E	S
A	R	E	O		A	H	O	M	E
S	A	L	T	S	H	A	K	E	R
P	L	A	T	A		T	O	R	I
		I	N	F		R	I	A	
P	E	P	P	E	R	M	I	L	L
U	N	L		R	A	O			
L	S	A	T		N	G	A	I	O
S	U	G	A	R	C	U	B	E	S
A	R	U	B	A		L	O	O	S
R	E	E	S	E		S	O	H	O

DUBIOUS DEFINITIONS (PAGE 194)

B	I	O		N	A	A	C	P
A	R	R		O	S	L	E	R
D	E	C	O	M	P	O	S	E
E	S	A	U			T	A	M
			T	I	N	O	R	E
D	E	B	R	I	E	F	E	D
A	R	R	E	S	T			
N	I	A			T	A	P	A
D	E	S	E	R	V	I	N	G
E	P	S	O	N		D	I	E
R	A	Y	E	D		A	N	S

ANSWERS

KNIVES OUT (PAGE 196)

A	S	A		M	O	M		S	I	R	E	E
T	E	X	T	U	R	E		K	N	O	T	S
A	R	O	U	S	E	S		I	D	E	A	L
D	A	N	I	E	L	C	R	A	I	G		
			L	E	S	A	B	R	E			
P	E	E	L		E	L	I	E		E	O	S
L	E	V	E	E			A	L	L	A	H	
O	L	E		P	A	B	A		I	F	F	Y
		M	I	N	I	C	A	B				
	B	E	S	T	A	C	T	R	E	S	S	
N	E	W	D	O		S	O	L	A	R	I	A
P	L	A	I	D		E	R	A	S	I	N	G
R	O	Y	C	E		D	D	S		E	K	E

TRUE DETECTIVE (PAGE 200)

S	E	R	G	E		M	I	M	I	C
H	E	A	R	N		A	P	A	C	E
A	R	C	E	D		C	O	H	O	S
D	O	H		U	S	A		E	N	T
		E	M	P	O	W	E	R		
O	N	L	O	A	N		A	S	T	A
T	E	M	P	T		A	S	H	E	N
C	E	C	E		G	U	Y	A	N	A
	A	D	R	E	N	A	L			
O	C	D		A	M	T		A	E	F
K	H	A	K	I		B	L	A	R	E
R	A	M	E	N		E	L	L	I	S
A	S	S	A	Y		E	D	I	C	T

DOOHICKEYS (PAGE 198)

AMERICAN SERIAL KILLERS (PAGE 202)

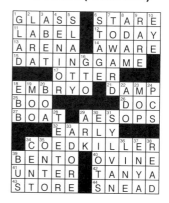

252

DIET CONSCIOUS (PAGE 204)

B	M	W		C	A	P		J	U	I	C	E
M	A	R		O	L	E		A	S	C	O	T
A	D	E		P	E	A		M	A	Y	B	E
J	E	N	N	Y	C	R	A	I	G			
	A	S	E	C			F	E	E	L	E	R
		H	A	N	O	I			I	R	A	
M	E	D	I	T	E	R	R	A	N	E	A	N
I	T	A			H	Y	E	N	A			
L	A	M	A	R	R			Y	M	C	A	
		S	O	U	T	H	B	E	A	C	H	
C	A	R	P	S		R	I	O		W	O	O
A	B	A	C	I		E	N	D		E	R	R
V	E	G	A	N		S	T	Y		D	N	A

FASHION FORWARD (PAGE 208)

O	W	L	S		A	B	E	S		V	E	T
R	I	O	T		D	U	D	E		E	W	E
C	L	A	I	B	O	R	N	E		R	E	X
A	D	D	L	E		E	A	R	H	A	R	T
			E	L	B	A		S	A	W		
N	A	G		T	O	U	R		Z	A	P	S
F	L	I	M	S	Y		H	A	Y	N	I	E
L	I	V	E		S	U	E	D		G	E	T
	E	A	R		N	A	I	L				
P	O	N	T	I	A	C		E	A	S	E	S
I	N	C		S	T	L	A	U	R	E	N	T
N	T	H		K	R	O	C		G	A	Z	A
S	O	Y		S	A	G	E		E	T	O	N

SHERLOCK (PAGE 206)

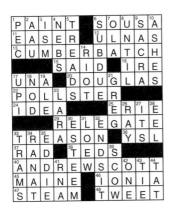

¹P	²A	³I	⁴N	⁵T		⁶S	⁷O	⁸U	⁹S	¹⁰A
¹¹E	A	S	E	R		¹²U	L	N	A	S
¹³C	U	M	B	E	¹⁴R	B	A	T	C	H
		¹⁵S	A	I	D		¹⁶I	R	E	
¹⁷U	¹⁸N	¹⁹A		²⁰D	O	²¹U	G	L	A	S
²²P	O	L	L	S	T	E	R			
²⁴I	D	E	A			²⁵E	²⁶R	²⁷I	²⁸E	
		²⁹R	E	³⁰L	³¹E	G	A	³²T	E	
³³T	³⁴R	E	A	S	O	N		³⁶Y	S	L
³⁷R	A	D		³⁸T	E	³⁹D	S			
⁴⁰A	N	⁴¹D	R	E	W	S	C	⁴²O	⁴³T	⁴⁴T
⁴⁵M	A	I	N	E		⁴⁶I	O	N	I	A
⁴⁷S	T	E	A	M		⁴⁸T	W	E	E	T

LEADING AMYS (PAGE 210)

S	T	O	M	P		S	M	U		A	L	L
L	O	R	R	E		K	E	G		M	I	A
A	M	Y	I	R	V	I	N	G		Y	E	T
T	E	X		S	A	M		A	R	G	U	E
			F	I	T		A	M	E	R		
T	R	A	L	A		U	N	S	N	A	R	L
L	I	M	A		A	M	Y		A	N	T	E
C	A	Y	M	A	N	S		O	T	T	E	R
		A	B	L	E		S	P	A			
C	A	D	E	T		L	E	A		P	I	T
I	R	A		A	M	Y	A	Q	U	I	N	O
T	I	M		R	E	L		U	S	U	R	Y
E	D	S		S	T	E		E	A	S	E	S

ANSWERS

ADAM DRIVER FILMS
(PAGE 212)

D	E	P	P		A	L	I		B	T	U	S
C	I	A	O		J	O	N		O	S	S	O
I	N	R	E		A	D	S	L	O	G	A	N
		T	H	E	R	E	P	O	R	T		
	C	E	L	S			A	W	S			
T	H	R	E	A	D	E	D			C	U	E
M	A	R	R	I	A	G	E	S	T	O	R	Y
I	R	E			R	O	S	E	W	I	N	E
		A	R	K			E	O	N	S		
	F	R	A	N	C	E	S	H	A			
I	C	A	N	T	E	L	L		O	B	O	E
W	I	K	I		S	A	L		U	L	N	A
O	G	E	E		S	P	Y		R	E	S	T

HAWAII FIVE-O (PAGE 216)

WOMEN OF ACTION
(PAGE 214)

T	O	M	B		B	B	S		J	U	T	E
A	D	I	A		R	A	T		U	P	O	N
L	E	N	T		U	R	E		L	I	D	O
C	R	I	M	I	N	A	L	M	I	N	D	S
		A	N	C		L	I	E				
C	R	U	N	C	H		A	C	C	R	U	E
S	U	R	F					H	A	T	S	
I	G	L	O	O	S		S	T	R	E	E	P
		R	C	A		P	O	I				
P	A	G	E	T	B	R	E	W	S	T	E	R
O	L	A	V		R	O	E		T	I	L	E
M	O	L	E		E	N	D		I	D	E	A
P	E	E	R		S	A	O		E	Y	E	D

254

ANSWERS

CUBIC ZIRCONIA (PAGE 218)

L	I	T	H	E		T	L	C		A	S	K
P	O	B	O	X		O	O	O		Q	U	I
G	U	S	T	O		M	A	R	Q	U	I	S
A	S	P		T	U	B		E	T	A	T	S
			T	I	S		E	R	R			
P	R	I	N	C	E	S	S			J	O	Y
J	I	L	T		D	E	C		O	A	H	U
S	O	L		T	E	A	R	D	R	O	P	
			S	F	O		P	O	D			
J	E	L	L	O		D	E	B		A	R	K
E	M	E	R	A	L	D		B	E	L	I	E
E	M	S		M	E	A		E	M	P	T	Y
R	Y	E		Y	A	Y		R	U	S	E	S

NCIS (PAGE 222)

W	H	I	S	T		B	A	N	A	L
S	I	N	C	E		I	H	O	P	E
J	E	T	H	R	O	G	I	B	B	S
			W	I	N	D		U	S	S
F	E	T	A		C	A	T			
A	V	A		R	E	D	C	A	P	E
H	E	T	T	Y		D	U	C	K	Y
D	R	I	V	E	B	Y		A	G	E
			S	S	E		H	I	S	S
A	W	S		E	L	S	E			
D	A	N	I	E	L	A	R	U	A	H
A	W	A	R	D		G	O	N	N	A
M	A	G	E	S		O	D	I	N	G

CHARLES MANSON (PAGE 220)

P	O	P	A	R	T		A	R	M	I	N	G
S	P	O	T	T	Y		N	O	M	A	Y	O
H	E	L	T	E	R	S	K	E	L	T	E	R
A	R	E	A		A	A	A		R	T	D	
W	A	R	B	O	N	D		P	R	O	S	Y
			O	U	T		M	A	A			
S	A	T	Y	R		F	E	L	T	B	A	D
A	L	I		O	W	N		T	U	B	A	
L	O	V	E	A	N	D	T	E	R	R	O	R
T	H	O	R	P	E		O	N	A	R	U	N
S	A	S	S	E	S		R	E	P	O	T	S

ANSWERS

MAGICAL WORLD OF TEA
(PAGE 224)

A	G	I	S	T		C	H	E	W	O	F	F
L	U	N	A		E	L	E	V		A	E	R
A	N	K	H		G	R	E	E	N	T	E	A
S	P	Y	I	N	G		D	N	A			
	O		B	A	I	O		T	I	D	A	L
K	W	A		S	E	A	M		L	I	F	E
E	D	S		A	S	S	A	M		L	T	V
R	E	E	K		T	I	R	E		L	E	O
F	R	A	U	D		S	L	A	M		R	
		D	O	S		E	T	E	R	N	E	
I	N	F	U	S	I	O	N		R	O	O	T
P	I	O		E	N	C	E		C	M	O	N
S	M	O	L	D	E	R		H	Y	E	N	A

NEW YEAR'S EVE
(PAGE 226)

H	A	R	M		C	C	C		C	H	I	C
U	V	E	A		A	Z	O		A	M	M	O
P	E	T	I	T	M	A	L		T	O	F	U
	C	E	L	E	B	R	A	T	E			N
F			L	T	R			E	R	E	C	T
I	M	H	O		I	M	A	X		B	O	D
R	O	U	T		A	R	N		H	A	L	O
E	N	G		S	N	I	T		A	N	E	W
W	A	H	O	O			I	G	G			N
O			C	H	A	M	P	A	G	N	E	
R	U	S	T		L	A	O	T	I	A	N	S
K	A	M	E		G	R	P		S	T	Y	E
S	E	P	T		A	X	E		H	O	A	X